THE LITURGY IN THE CATECHISM

THE LITURGY
IN THE CATECHISM

Celebrating God's Wisdom and Love

Regis A. Duffy OFM

**GEOFFREY
CHAPMAN**

Geoffrey Chapman
A Cassell imprint
Wellington House, 125 Strand, London WC2R 0BB
215 Park Avenue South, New York, NY 10003

© Regis A. Duffy OFM 1995

First published 1995

British Library Cataloguing-in-Publication Data
A catalogue record for this book is available from the British Library.

ISBN 0-225-66790-8

Typeset by York House Typographic Ltd
Printed and bound in Great Britain by Biddles Ltd, Guildford and King's Lynn

Contents

Introduction

THIS SMALL BOOK has quite modest goals. It was written in response to a request for a non-specialist commentary on the liturgical theology of the 'Sacramental Economy' section of the *Catechism of the Catholic Church*. It attempts to provide some of the theological context for the highly condensed and finely tuned exposition of the Catechism. The section on the seven sacraments in the Catechism has supplied examples for some of the teaching on the liturgy. The text of the Catechism is cited in this book by the paragraph number in parentheses. The notes at chapter ends have been restricted to the most essential citations.

I hope that this brief commentary might encourage those who have the privilege of celebrating, preaching, and teaching the worship of the Church to carry on their gospel tasks with new insight and renewed commitment.

I wish to thank Michael Walsh for initiating this project.

Regis A. Duffy OFM
Scholar in Residence, The Franciscan Institute
St Bonaventure University, New York, USA

1

Celebrated wisdom

WHETHER WE LIKE classical or hard rock music, we expect musicians to perform, not simply to talk about the music. This does not mean that we consider their training and knowledge of the music to be unimportant but rather that we want to experience music performed with skill and insight. Catechesis and liturgy are the music of conversion. They are meant to be lived, not simply studied or ritualized. As with music, this is not to say that the study of the faith and its liturgical enactment are unimportant, but to remind ourselves of theology's ultimate purpose – the living of the gospel life. Since this book deals with liturgy within a catechetical context, it is important at the very outset to spell out some of the assumptions and connections between these two areas.

In this opening chapter, five assumptions will be briefly explained since they will also form part of the discussion in later chapters. The first assumption is that catechetics, along with evangelization and liturgy, is always a companion to conversion. The second assumption is that the teaching and preaching of liturgy must reflect the mission and praxis of the local as well as the universal Church. A third assumption is that the teaching and celebration of what Christ has done for us is always done within a specific cultural context which must be taken into account. A fourth supposition is that the gospel message and the worship of the Church demand the response of the whole human person. Finally, liturgy continues to be a source of insight and wisdom for the evangelizing and praying Church. Before commenting on these assumptions, a few words should be said about learning models in the Christian community.

Learning models

There is currently a great deal of criticism of post-conciliar catechetics, principally because younger people do not seem to 'know' details of Christian doctrine with the precision that their parents did. With the advent of Vatican II, religious educators critically reassessed the pre-conciliar catechetics and found it to be wanting in several areas. As a result, more experiential and interactive models of learning and celebrating the faith were proposed. While these evaluations and methods were not perfect, they did represent a contemporary understanding of the classsical catechumenal model in which celebrating and learning the faith were intimately connected.

The catechumenate was an extended period of training to live the gospel life. The great catechumenal teachers, such as Tertullian, Ambrose and Augustine, remain some of the great theologians of the Church. In other words, they saw no opposition between an intellectual training in the faith and an intense challenge to live the faith. In contemporary language, we would say that this approach attempted to address the whole person. Tertullian, the committed Christian teacher in the catechumenate in Carthage, North Africa, reminds both the catechumens and the baptized of his time about the link between hearing and living God's word:

> Let no one flatter himself, therefore, that because he is classed among the auditors in the catechumenate, he is, on that account, still permitted to sin ... We are not baptized so that we may cease committing sin but because we have ceased ... This, surely, is the first Baptism of the catechumen.[1]

The catechumenal model, then, encourages a learning and liturgy that bears fruit in gospel living. The Catechism expresses a similar goal 'to reveal in all clarity the joy and the demands of the way of Christ' (1697).

Liturgy and catechesis in dialogue

To develop the fundamental assumption that catechesis and liturgy are complementary dimensions of ongoing experience of conversion we must first look at what we mean by conversion. In popular usage, when we say that someone 'converted', we often mean that they have changed their affiliation from one denomination to another. This is not the biblical understanding of conversion.

Conversion, in the scriptural sense, is the radical reorientation of one's life acccording to God's values and purposes. The Catechism expresses it in this way: 'Interior repentance is the radical reorientation of one's whole life . . . it entails the desire and resolution to change one's life . . .' (1431). Our lives are shaped, in part, by the goals we set for ourselves and the things that we prize. One of the most common effects of radical sin in the world is the tendency to set our hearts on lesser values and short-range goals. In the rush of daily living, we can too readily accept these guideposts without critically reassessing them. The examples of conversion in the Catechism point to the concerns and values that modern living does not necessarily promote: gestures of reconciliation, concern for the poor, the exercise and defence of justice and the rights of the alienated and marginal, and so on (1435). A realistic pastoral translation of this warning might be found in the audiovisual world of young people. Many of the implicit values and life choices proposed there are hostile to those of the gospel, not only in the area of sex and drugs but also in terms of rampant consumerism and selfish lifestyles. In view of the force of the cultural tides of our time conversion is not an easy matter.

Knowledge of our faith and attendance at worship do not ncessarily lead to a critical reassessment of our lifestyle and values. This is why our way of teaching the faith and our participation in worship must constantly be measured by the ongoing conversion in our own lives and in that of our local Christian community. (We will develop some of these ideas in Chapter 2.) For the moment, we can sum up this point by saying that learning the gospel way and praising God in Christ through the Spirit are experiences tied to our ongoing acceptance of all that Christ has done for us. These experiences of God's healing presence in the life of the Church and its individuals, celebrated with praise and thanksgiving in the liturgy, have gradually been clarified. This is one of the meanings of the classical axiom, 'The law of worship establishes the law of belief' (a point we will return to a number of times). Saving doctrine is never separated from the saving experience of God that grounds our faith and its expression in worship.

The living Church

Although we will discuss the connection between the Church and liturgy in the next chapter, we must say a word now about the actual living practice of the Church. The teaching and preaching of liturgy must reflect the mission and praxis of the local as well as the universal Church. The terms 'local Church' and 'praxis' require some clarification. The 'local Church' refers to a specific group of Christians gathered by the word of God around their bishop and nourished by the sacraments in order to bear witness to the gospel message.[2] (A diocese might be considered a local Church.) The 'universal Church' denotes a communion of such Churches.

There are theoretical or doctrinal descriptions of the Church which present the ideal, uncomplicated by a particular historical period or a specific culture. But Christians worship and appropriate the faith within a living community called the local Church which is affected, for better and worse, by a specific historical and cultural context. Therefore, it is especially important to situate any discussion of the Church and its liturgy in both its universal and its local contexts. The 'practice' (sometimes called 'praxis' from the Greek word 'to do') refers to the way in which our ideas and ideals interact with our living. In other words, it is the actual implementation of a belief whether or not it is correct.

Thus, the gospel and theology propose the way Christian life is to be lived while the history of the Church describes some aspects of the practice or living out of that ideal in specific eras. Paul, for example, in 1 Corinthians contrasts the theology of the eucharist with the conflicting praxis of the local (i.e. Corinthian) Church. Paul reminds the Corinthians of the redemptive unity that the eucharist makes possible and contrasts it with the actual divisions in their community. The biblical image of praxis is 'a tree bearing good fruit', that is, an authentic living out of one's belief. It is vitally important for theologians and pastoral ministers to keep examining the practice as well as the theory of Christian life as lived out in a particular Church.

At present, the Church has had more than three decades of living experience since Vatican II. Local Churches have had to implement the liturgical changes of the Council during a time in which both the ordained ministries and religious communities have lost an important number of their members. The active role of the Church in matters of justice and peace has, in some countries, caused division and even persecution. While the majority of Catholics seem to have welcomed the liturgical reforms of Vatican II, there are still enclaves hostile to the conciliar changes. In some dioceses and parishes, these divisions are still a source of pastoral tension and liturgical disagreement. Some parishes, for example, may have one style of Mass to satisfy more conservative parishioners and another for those welcoming a more participatory liturgy.

Paul VI in his letter 'On Evangelization' also reminded the Church that the gospel is not proclaimed in a vacuum. He urged local Churches to be aware of the local, social and cultural contexts which help or hinder the practice or the living of the gospel that is proclaimed. Culture is the sum total of explicit and implicit values and visions of a particular society. When the Church has lost this cultural awareness in a particular time or situation, she has always found it difficult to speak to people in a prophetic way. When, for example, the particular cultural use of Latin in worship became a fixed and universal law for the Western Church, it distanced liturgical celebrations and their challenging meanings from peoples whose cultural heritage no longer included the Latin language. The Catechism has emphasized the importance of its teaching being adapted to particular situations (24).

One of the most pervasive examples of culture is language, for it carries the attitudes of a people about the meaning and purpose of life. American English, for example, differs from British English not simply because of word usage, spelling, or different vocabulary (e.g., 'truck' or 'lorry') but because two cultures with different perspectives are in play. Some social commentators have noted how the use of language reinforces a particular approach to values. Social groups that value well-defined codes of behaviour may use a 'restricted' speech code ('Do it because I tell you!') while more 'liberal' groups may employ an 'elaborated' speech code ('Let me explain why I want you to take out the garbage').[3] When people of either persuasion celebrate the liturgy, they will usually bring with them these same codes. In listening to a homily, one group might object that the homilist was not restrictive enough in his discussion of a moral question while the other might have wished for a more nuanced presentation that allowed for the complexities of living the gospel in the modern world. (We shall discuss some of these cultural issues again in the final chapter.)

Since the gospel presents God's values and vision, it must enter into dialogue with the host culture. Paul VI gives the reasons for this dialogue. People who hear the gospel have also heard a specific cultural message since their birth. One might say that we hear the gospel with our acculturated ears. The Pope concludes: ' ... the kingdom which the gospel proclaims is lived by men who are profoundly linked to a culture, and the building up of the kingdom cannot avoid borrowing the elements of human culture or cultures'.[4] Not only must evangelization employ the language of a culture, it must also uncover God's creative work in that culture and must confront attitudes and values that distort that work.

The point of this short digression on culture was to give some background for the assertion that the practice as well as the theory of liturgy must be discussed. The practice of the liturgy since Vatican II is like Joseph's coat of many colours. The sociocultural situation of Great Britain or France provided a different context for the reception of Vatican II's liturgical reforms from that of the United States. To state the theory of liturgical celebration and participation without taking into account the actual situation and reception of the reforms by English or American Catholics would be naive, if not deceptive. Both the catechetical and the liturgical teaching, for example, on the eucharist in recent years have rightly emphasized the aspects of the eucharist as a meal. But the fast-food culture and the social phenomenon of both parents working have made the experience of the shared meal a rushed if not rare experience for many families in some English-speaking countries. From a cultural viewpoint, the meal is no longer the shared experience that it was fifty years ago. In speaking of the eucharist as meal, the catechist and liturgist must take into account the actual experience of their listeners. Any discussion of liturgy that hopes to have some pastoral effect must also take this cultural tension into account.

An embodied participation

'Participation' is a key word in any discussion of liturgy (as we shall see in Chapter 4). For the moment, participation can be described as responsive and responsible worship that deepens our commitment to the reign of God. From Paul's use of the Greek term *koinōnia* and its repeated use in the prayers of the Roman liturgy to Vatican II's frequent allusions the concern about how the human person takes part in worship has been a constant refrain. This concern is shown in the way in which Paul not only informs his converts about Christ but also urges them to imitate him.[5] This same approach is present when the great catechumenal teachers invite their converts to enter into the mystery being revealed. Augustine, for example, explains the phrase 'Body of Christ' which the newly baptized have heard on receiving their first eucharist in this way: 'Be what you see (Body of Christ), receive what you are (the Body of Christ).'[6] Augustine's urging to 'be' and 'receive' are not simply addressed to the mind but to the whole Christian person acting as well as believing. Participation in worship always involves the whole person.

We have already mentioned that one of the post-conciliar changes in catechetics was an attempt to return to this classic emphasis on Christian formation in worship as an experience involving both mind and heart. In the nineteenth century there had been a need to counteract the rationalism of the period by describing faith (as Vatican I, in fact, did) in relation to our ability to find God with our reason. Vatican II, after repeating this definition, then offered a more biblical description of faith as the gift of our whole self freely to God.[7]

Even a cursory glance at this definition of faith will cue the reader about how demanding this notion of belief is. Both theologians and social commentators lament the difficulties of being 'a whole person' in the increasingly department-alized living of the late twentieth century. The working lives, for example, of many people are completely separated from their worship. In fact, worship may often be used to escape the realities of the working week. And what of Vatican II's mention of 'freely' giving our whole self? In our post-industrial societies that are frequently pictured as narcissistic and self-preoccupied, how 'free' are the people who step into a church after a week of living in such situations?[8] Since fruitful liturgy and sacramental participation must reflect the operational definitions of participants' faith, these questions merit some honest answers.

The classical liturgy of the Church has always had this potential for helping Christians to respond on all the levels of their personality. Liturgical silence, for example, in the celebration of the eucharist (after the call to pray and again after the readings, for example) allows a place for the non-verbal dimension of our response. In trains and buses one may be aware of a sterile silence that results from an anonymous and even fear-filled situation. In some homes, only a hostile silence is known. By contrast, an attentive and healing silence in the presence of God periodically in the liturgy helps us to discover how large the 'whole person' is. In more solemn celebrations, the silent actions of the elevation and the incensing of the scriptures invite a reverence that is more than intellectual. Although there is still a tendency in some liturgical celebrations to give pride of place to the verbal dimension ('When in doubt, say something!'), the post-conciliar liturgical reforms do try to foster our affective as well as intellectual responses by offering options (such as different ways of expressing our sorrow for sin in the sacrament of penance and reconciliation).

But our earlier discussion of the cultural context for hearing God's word and worshipping should remind us that embodied participation also has a cultural dimension. In many post-industrial cultures, people are often conditioned to be aware of their bodies only when sexually aroused, ill, or in socially unacceptable or threatening situations. Certain rituals, therefore, that might be perfectly acceptable in a Mediterranean culture (such as embracing at the sign of peace) might not be so easily appropriated in Anglo-Saxon cultures. A sensitive catechetical liturgy selects ritual expressions which have some root in the culture and then gives a new dimension of meaning to them (think of the handshake at the sign of peace). Even some of the differences between the liturgical explanations of Ambrose in Milan and Cyril in Jerusalem to catechumens may reflect the cultural as well as the historical situation of their local Churches. Ambrose of Milan, for example, explains the pre-baptismal anointing by a reference to the anointing of athletes while Cyril of Jerusalem sees the same anointing as pointing to the candidate's participation in the true olive tree, Jesus Christ.[9]

Another dimension of a more total liturgical participation is the personal narrative of how God has constantly touched the life of this person. We learn and ritualize out of our experience. But the Christian's awareness of this redemptive experience is often fragmentary and edited. As a result, their praise and thanks to God for the unearned gift of redemption is sometimes more theoretical than experienced. Individuals' awareness of their own spiritual autobiography does not privatize the public worship of the Church but rather links individuals more deeply by this shared experience of God's redemptive love. As in the case of the other assumptions previewed in this chapter, we will develop in later chapters this idea of how the personal experience of God's saving presence and the public character of worship complement each other.

God teaches through worship

The classic axiom about the law of worship establishing the law of belief has already been mentioned above. There are several levels of meaning to this axiom. For the moment, we need only attend to one of these meanings: through the liturgy God teaches us, both individually and communally, our profound redemptive need as well as the power of Christ's dying and rising for us that is the basis of our knowing and praising God.

Any good teacher knows that one obstacle to learning is a student's conviction that he or she already adequately knows a particular topic. An important element in the art of teaching is to help students discover their ignorance so that the process of learning can continue. Jesus used the parable in this pedagogical way. His audience thought that they knew enough about the reign of God, but Jesus' parables disconcerted his listeners by revealing the depth and width of God's plan and their place in it. As a result, they began to learn again.

In liturgy God continues to teach us our profound redemptive need, not in universal terms ('Every human being needs redemption') but in the autobiographical terms briefly discussed above. A classic example is the autobiography of St Augustine where he learns that in reviewing the often banal details of earlier chapters of his life, he finds the saving action of God as well as the deeper personal strengths and weaknesses that necessitated God's presence. The result of these insights is a new urgency and gratitude in his prayer and worship. In similar fashion, our re-examined lives will always yield new insights about our profound need and God's continuing healing. This new awareness transforms our familiar rituals of worship from polite acknowledgement of God's work in our lives to a more urgent praise and thanks.

Liturgy is, first of all, a complex experience, for it deals with the mystery of God as well as our response to that mystery. In the next chapter, we will examine how the Catechism begins to lay the groundwork for a realistic notion of what our praise and thanks to God will entail.

Notes

1 Tertullian, *On Penitence* in *Treatises on Penance*, trans. W. LeSaint (Westminster, MD: Newman, 1959), pp. 24, 25–6.

2 For a perceptive discussion, see R. McBrien, *Catholicism* (San Francisco: HarperSanFrancisco/London: Geoffrey Chapman, 1994), pp. 724–30. In the documents of Vatican II, the local Church is usually referred to as a 'particular church' (e.g., chapter 3 of the Decree on the Church's Missionary Activity, *Ad Gentes*).

3 See M. Douglas, *Natural Symbols* (New York: Pantheon, 1970), pp. 23–36.

4 Paul VI, *On Evangelization* 20.1, in *Proclaiming Justice and Peace: Documents from John XXIII to John Paul II* (1984), ed. M. Walsh and B. Davies (Mystic, CT: Twenty-Third Publications/London: Collins, 1984), p. 213.

5 For a discussion of the importance of 'imitation' in the rhetoric of Paul's day, see M. M. Mitchell, *Paul and the Rhetoric of Reconciliation* (Louisville, KY: Westminster/John Knox, 1991), pp. 49–60.

6 Augustine, *Sermon* 272.

7 Vatican II, *Dei Verbum* (Dogmatic Constitution on Divine Revelation) 5: in *Vatican Council II: Conciliar and Post-Conciliar Documents*, ed. A. Flannery (Dublin: Dominican Publications/Northport, NY: Costello, 1988), p. 752.

8 See John Coleman, 'Values and virtues in advanced modern societies' in *Changing Values and Virtues*, ed. D. Mieth and J. Pohier (Edinburgh: T. & T. Clark, 1987), pp. 3–13.

9 Ambrose of Milan, *On the Sacraments* I, 4: with Fr. trans. in *Des Sacrementis, Des Mystères, Explication du Symbole*, ed. B. Botte (Sources

Chrétiennes 25bis; Paris: Cerf, 1961); Cyril of Jerusalem, *Mystagogical Catechesis* II, 3: with Fr. trans. in *Catéchèses Mystagogiques*, ed. A. Piédagnel (Sources Chrétiennes 126bis; Paris: Cerf, 1988), p. 109. *Pace* A. Chupungco, *Beyond Inculturation* (Washington, DC: Pastoral Press, 1994), p. 9.

2

To love a mystery

COMPLEX EXPERIENCES LIKE love and genius are
notoriously difficult to define because they have many dimensions. 'Liturgy' is another example of an experience difficult
to define. The Catechism, in the beginning of its discussion
on the liturgy, offers some initial hints for such a definition.
The Church proclaims the mystery of Christ in its liturgy
where 'the work of our redemption is accomplished' (1067).
The meaning of the Greek root of 'liturgy' ('a public work/
service on behalf of the people') and its transposed Christian
meaning as 'participation of the People of God in "the work
of God"' are also mentioned (1069).

But the authors of this section of the Catechism are well
aware that much more must be included in such a definition.
Such a definition might be like a mosaic with its many
individual pieces contributing to the total picture. This chapter deals with some of the dimensions that make up the
richness and beauty of the liturgical experience. How is the
Trinity both the cause and the focus of our worship? What is
Christ's participation in that prayer? How do the notions of
paschal mystery and sin heighten our appreciation of liturgy?
Does the Church, understood as a credible 'communion'
and a prophetic witness, have anything to do with our celebrations? The answers to these questions should enhance our
definitions and celebrations of liturgy.

Saving names

In the history of art, the depiction of the Holy Trinity is a fascinating study in itself. Not only children but many adults picture the Father as an older individual with a beard, Christ as crucified, and the Holy Spirit as a bird. There are other artistic traditions such as imaging the Trinity as three young men. For all that, Christianity has always recognized the inadequacy of picturing God in the arts or in words. God's inner life, although much written about in theology, remains a mystery that will not be exhausted even in eternity. Liturgy and the scriptures were the first, and remain the best, teachers of theology about the Trinity. It should not be surprising, then, that the Catechism begins its discussion of liturgy with the mystery of the Holy Trinity (1066). Yet it is only in recent years that liturgical theologians have called for a more extended recognition of this mystery in the worship of the Church.[1]

In the past, Western theology has usually discussed the Trinity in abstract philosophical terms. This trend developed because of the need to combat heresies about the nature of God with clear philosophical categories. The liturgy, however, keys its praise and thanks not only to the God who exists but to the God who saves.[2] The Catechism sums up this perspective by saying that 'the Father accomplishes the "mystery of his will" by giving his beloved Son and his Holy Spirit for the salvation of the world and for the glory of his name' (1066).[3] The wisdom of this approach is that it mirrors the way in which every human being has first encountered not the God of the philosophers but a saving God. One theologian has expressed it in this way: 'We do not have a direct knowledge of God's "inner being", but only of God's self-revelation in the works of creation, in the person of Jesus and in the ongoing presence of the Spirit.'[4] The God of this view is called the 'economic' Trinity (the Greek word in the New Testament for the 'plan of salvation'). For those who evangelize and catechize, this approach also provides a dynamic way in which to present a truth that is at the heart of our Christian faith.

Paul gives an example of this 'economic' approach when he speaks of Jesus as the Son of God and as the crucified one: 'Whatever promises God has made have been fulfilled in him; therefore, it is through him that we address our Amen to God when we worship together' (2 Cor 1:16). In other words, Christ as saviour provides the frame in which we view and worship the God whose promises of salvation have been fulfilled.

But the observant reader will no doubt respond that this citation does not deal with the Trinity since there is no mention of the Holy Spirit. Yet, as Catherine LaCugna points out, 'The Holy Spirit is almost never mentioned explicitly, yet the early church was very much aware of the Spirit. Its life was the life *of* the Spirit'.[5] This is readily apparent when she cites the praise-prayers that dot the letters of Paul, as in this passage: 'Do everything in the name of the Lord Jesus, giving thanks to God the Father through him' (Col 3:17).[6] The liturgy never forgets that God through Christ in the Spirit has saved us, and the New Testament reflects that same awareness.[7] The Catechism, as we will see shortly, reminds us that with baptism we enter into the life of the Trinity (1240). Theology will eventually articulate this same message of Paul as does the liturgy: the Spirit that anointed Jesus for service also anoints the Christian for that same purpose.

An early example of such awareness can be found in the *Didache*, a work some scholars date to the late New Testament period.[8] In the prayers in chapters 9 and 10 (which may be table prayers or a eucharistic prayer), thanks is given to the Father over the cup and the bread for the mystery of salvation ('for the holy vine of David your servant') and 'for the life and knowledge which you have revealed to us through Jesus your *Child*'. The Greek word *pais*, translated here as 'Child', has two meanings, 'son' and 'servant' as does its Hebrew counterpart, *ebed*. Other liturgies contain the same expression, for example, that of Hippolytus' *Apostolic Tradition*. (Later liturgies use the unambiguous word *huios* that can only mean 'child/son'.) The prayer proclaims 'glory be yours through all ages' for the servant whose blood sealed the Father's new covenant. For this reason he has been 'made Son of God in power ... by his resurrection from the dead' (Rom 1:4). In other words, the liturgy uses this double meaning (son/ servant) to connect the Father and the Son in the shared task of our redemption.[9]

Less familiar, perhaps, to some readers is the notion that all creation is the result of Trinitarian love (257–258). The connection between creation and redemption can be summed up in the axiom – what the Trinity creates the Trinity redeems.[10] This principle will be especially important in future chapters for understanding visible signs of creation in the liturgy and in the sacraments. For the moment, it is enough to recall how early Christian prayer brings together a basic recognition that creation and Trinity are linked: 'We give you thanks, O God, through your beloved Child (*pais*) Jesus Christ, whom you have sent us in the last days ... he is your Word, inseparable from you, through whom you have created everything ...'[11]

Before speaking of how the catechumenal process inculcated this approach in its candidates, we should make some contemporary connections. If the mystery of the Holy Trinity has remained on the periphery of popular Christian awareness, it may be because philosophical approaches have obscured the redemptive approach to this mystery. Therefore, it is important to remember that both candidates and the baptized already have an extended experience with the saving presence of the Holy Trinity in their own lived experience. Without such a presence, even the first steps of conversion would be impossible.[12]

But Christians must be made aware of this saving history in their own lives. The classical model for this retrieval is spiritual autobiography (such as of St Augustine or St Teresa of Avila) in which we rediscover the footprints of God in our lives. This model relies on the questions by which we re-examine what God has done in our lives. Honest answers to such questions inevitably elicit our praise and thanks to the Trinity.

The Trinity has indeed accompanied us at every moment of life's journey. Like the inexperienced observer standing before a canvas of Turner or Van Gogh, we may initially only see a few of the colours in that subtle and complex interplay of our lives and God's action there. Gradually we discover what we had at first missed – all the other occasions which prompt our deepened praise and wonder. The Catechism has already taught what the Trinity has done and is doing for us. It now draws out the corollary of this teaching: 'Liturgy is also the participation in Christ's own prayer addressed to the Father in the Holy Spirit ... Through the liturgy the inner man is rooted and grounded in "the great love with which [the Father] loved us" in his beloved Son' (1073).

Speaking of the unspeakable

We can always learn from effective teachers. Among such teachers in the history of Christianity are scores of known and unknown catechumenal mentors who led their candidates through the stages of conversion and evangelization. The recognition of how God entered human lives was at the core of their teaching. The effectiveness of their teaching was eventually tested in the witness of the catechumens' lives as much as by the final questions they were asked just before their baptism. In the catechumenates of the second to the fourth centuries, these teachers were keenly aware that their students might be called to witness their faith in blood long before they could be asked the baptismal questions about the Trinity. Although we do not have texts for these earlier catechumenal instructions, it is certainly not difficult to reconstruct the commitment these doctrines were expected to evoke from the candidates. When the threat of persecution ceased, the great catechumenal teachers of the fourth and fifth centuries had, paradoxically, a more difficult situation in which to teach, but they met the challenge. Not only did conversion seem to demand less heroic witness from the fourth century on, there were now distinct social and political advantages to becoming a Christian. The catechumenal teachers had to know how to present the faith as an ongoing process of conversion whose doctrines did not excuse from but rather elicited commitment to the crucified Lord.

The Catechism itself provides a wonderful example in citing St Gregory of Nazianzus, speaking to his catechumens at Constantinople of the Trinity:

> Above all guard for me this great deposit of faith for which I live and fight, which I want to take with me as a companion, and which makes me bear all evils and despise all pleasures: I mean the profession of faith in the Father and the Son and the Holy Spirit. I entrust it to you today. (256)

What is particularly striking about Gregory's teaching is the tone of commitment with which he presents the teaching on the Holy Trinity.[13] While Gregory does not neglect doctrinal precision, he is convinced that this teaching must have an impact on these catechumens' lives in the world in which they find themselves.

In similar fashion, Ambrose, in explaining the three inter-rogations about the Trinity accompanying immersion in the baptismal waters and the consequent forgiveness of sins, points to Peter who was asked three times by Christ if the apostle loved him. Ambrose comments on Peter's and the catechumens' response: 'It is then the Father who forgives as well the Son and the Holy Spirit ... It is in that name (the Trinity) that you have all been saved, that you have been given the grace of life.'[14] Enrico Mazza has suggested that the teachers of this era spoke to their catechumens, taking into account the situation in which they found themselves.[15] They were convinced that the doctrine they taught was saving in every way, not only intellectually but morally and affectively. In speaking of John Chrysostom, Mazza says: 'In his eyes, the symbolism speaks of realities and not simply of meanings, *and is intended to give an experience* of the mystical content present in every rite.'[16] At the heart of this symbolic experience was the mystery of the death and resurrection of Jesus which revealed in turn the economic Trinity of which we have been speaking.

Speaking of mystery

There are any number of familiar terms (such as 'a black hole' in outer space or the 'window of opportunity') whose meanings we assume we know until actually challenged to define them. We then may discover that our understanding of a term was unclear, if not incorrect. 'Paschal mystery' is probably one such term for many people. Since Vatican II the expression has been repeated in homilies, religious education classes, and in the liturgy. The Catechism cites Vatican II when recalling how Christ accomplished our salvation 'principally by the Paschal mystery of his blessed Passion, Resurrection from the dead and glorious Ascension ...' (1067, citing the Decree on the Liturgy 5, 2) and later, in explaining the triple immersion of baptism, notes that 'it signifies and actually brings about death to sin and entry into the life of the Most Holy Trinity through configuration *to the Paschal mystery of Christ*' (1240). As familiar as it might sound, I have heard many a student in graduate theological courses who had difficulty in defining 'paschal mystery'. Yet the term is shorthand for how God has saved us.

'Mystery' has several current meanings, none of which comes near Paul's idea. For him, 'mystery' is the dynamic and saving presence of God in human history, whether we are aware of it or not. 'Paschal mystery' describes how God has saved us through Christ's self-gift on the cross. God has validated this self-gift in the resurrection and ascension of Christ. Paul and his contemporaries assume that no one can approach the mystery of God indifferently. One will come away better or worse for the encounter.

When Paul reminds the Corinthian Christians that 'Christ our Passover has been sacrificed' (1 Cor 5:7), he uncovers the meaning of our term.[17] 'Paschal' refers to Passover, the feast commemorating God saving the covenant people. The heart of the Passover is the sacrifice that unites the people with

God, the covenant sacrifice. In one line Paul forcefully implies that these former covenants no longer have value, because Christ's death for us is the basis of our union with God. We are a new covenant people. In his celebrated *Homily on the Pasch*, Melito of Sardis (second century) evokes this Pauline image: '... the figure has become the reality, and the lamb has become the Son, and the sheep has become a Man, and the Man has become God. Born as Son, led like a lamb, sacrificed like a sheep, buried as a man, he rises from the dead as God, being by nature both God and man.'[18]

Liturgy, however, in celebrating this mystery, also reminds us of a problem: Was this really necessary?

A different view

In worship we praise and thank God for the gift of salvation. But the implicit question remains – salvation from what? In our contemporary world, we recognize evil actions on the part of individuals and groups (e.g., the Holocaust, drug culture) as well as world-views which can sometimes corrupt a culture or a group for a period of time. For many, this situation is summed up by saying that this is not a perfect world. This sort of evaluation does not cry out for a redeemer because it assumes that if people would only try harder, things would not only be better, they would be fine.

But the paschal mystery suggests a very different assessment of our situation: faced with a flawed human nature as well as an imperfect world, there was nothing we could do to correct the situation if left to our own initiative. The Catechism points to God's solution, the two dimensions of the paschal mystery: the death of Jesus as liberation from sin and his resurrection as opening up the way to new life (654). Through baptism, the Christian receives the gift of the paschal mystery: we are made righteous and by the power of the Holy Spirit enabled to take part in his death by our dying to sin and in his resurrection by entering God's new life (1987–1988). Because this dying and rising is the very basis of our liturgical participation, it deserves some explanation.

For Paul the cross highlights our impossible situation: there was nothing we could do to please God before Christ's death. The apostle reminds his readers that even when people did try to keep God's law, they could never actually fulfil it. The irony of the situation was that people thought their own righteousness or good works to be the answer. Paul refers to his own experience before he recognized Christ as saviour: 'I was a Pharisee and so zealous that I persecuted the Church. I was above reproach when it came to justice based on the law' (Phil 3:5–6). In brief, this sinful situation of disobedience and separation from God preceded even our personal sins.

Paul describes Christ's death in terms of obedience to God, the first one in human history to be perfectly open to God's will and purpose. To emphasize his point, he uses an older liturgical hymn ('He was known to be of human estate, and it was thus that he humbled himself, obediently accepting even death') but adds a phrase of his own, 'death on a cross' (Phil 2:7c–8). The scandal of this added phrase for Paul's contemporaries is difficult for us to appreciate, but as the great Roman orator Cicero remarked, no one in the polite society of his time even mentioned such a death. Paul, however, wishes to emphasize how radical God's solution to our situation was.[19] With Christ's death everything is changed for the former Pharisee: 'I have been crucified with Christ and the life I live now is not my own ... I still live my human life, but it is a life of faith in the Son of God, who loved me and gave himself for me ... If justice is available through the law, then Christ died to no purpose' (Gal 2:19–21).

Paul's conviction is that only because of Christ's death is it possible to believe, to hope, and to love as God always intended. Commenting on these verses, one exegete says: '... Paul sees the cross at the heart of the story of Jesus. The cross not only marks the transition from old world to new creation ... but also sets the pattern for Christian conduct as self-giving love ... the Spirit whose lead the Galatians must follow is the Spirit of the crucified.'[20]

The phrase 'the paschal mystery', then, sums up the mystery of sin and the joy of redemption. For Paul this is no abstract theological idea but an experience which shapes our lives as well as our words of praise. As a result, we cannot use the flawed situation of our world and its people as an excuse for not becoming one with God and one another. For creation and its people are now a 'new creation': 'May I never boast of anything but the cross of our Lord Jesus Christ! Through it the world has been crucified to me and I to the world. It means nothing whether one is circumcised or not. All that matters is that one is created anew' (Gal 6:14–15). Paul is a realist who knows that evil has not disappeared. What has changed is our ability to be open to God and one another as Christ. When Paul looks at Christ he sees the ideal human being as God intended us all to be. The practical corollary he draws from a crucified Christ is also realistic: 'He died for all so that those who live might live no longer for themselves but for him who for their sakes died and was raised up' (2 Cor 5:15).[21]

Notice how Paul brings together themes that are still unconnected for others: radical sin in the world, the cross as the beginning of a new creation in us, the moral life as modelled on the cross, and all these themes finding their expression and clarification in worshipping the God who alone brought this about through Christ in the Spirit. Notice also that Paul speaks out of an experience, not simply an intellectual knowledge, of the paschal mystery. As already suggested, the catechist and homilist should follow this example.

No one is lacking experience of 'darkness' in his or her own life. This powerful biblical metaphor captures the situation of a flawed world and its people. When people, young or old, are asked about how the cross has touched that darkness in their lives, they may be startled at the question, but they are capable of eventually giving an answer. As mentioned earlier, a Paul or Augustine prays out of this renewed awareness of God's footprints in their lives. Authentic worship brings us back to our lives with new awareness of God's presence there.

Liturgy teaches us how to connect prayer and living, a connection that is constantly remarked in the life of Christ. The Catechism takes this same view: 'The liturgy is also a participation in Christ's own prayer addressed to the Father in the Holy Spirit. In the liturgy, all Christian prayer finds its source and goal. Through the liturgy the inner man is rooted and grounded in "the great love with which [the Father] loved us" in his beloved Son' (1073). The paschal mystery is at the heart of all conversion.

Doing the dance

Although there are books about dancing, it is meant to be performed, not to be read about. Conversion is much the same. It is not enough intellectually to understand and even assent to God's message: like the dance, conversion must be actively entered into. In Chapter 1 our first assumption was that catechesis, evangelization and liturgy are always companions to conversion. The Catechism put it this way: ' "The sacred liturgy does not exhaust the entire activity of the Church": it must be preceded by evangelization, faith and conversion' (1072). Our discussion of the paschal mystery certainly implies a radical change if we are to enter into the death and resurrection of Christ. But what does conversion mean in the late twentieth century?

Paul VI in his powerful letter *On Evangelization* spoke of conversion as the goal of evangelization: 'The Church evangelizes when she seeks to convert, solely through the divine power of the message she proclaims, both the personal and collective consciences of people, the activities in which they engage, and the lives and concrete milieux which are theirs.'[22] The Catechism expresses the same ideas in more general and biblical terms: change of heart, the reorientation of one's life, and turning from evil (1430–1432). (Some practical examples of conversion in daily life are also suggested in 1435.) But the point is always the same: conversion is a process that does not end until the moment of death. The

Catechism quite effectively describes this process by narrating the parable of the prodigal son (1439).

A classical model of conversion was restored to the Church by the post-conciliar reforms – the process of the catechumenate. (This process was mentioned in Chapter 1 as an example of formation in the faith that addressed both the mind and the heart.) This model was developed in the second-century Christian communities of Rome, Carthage and other centres in the Roman Empire to prepare candidates for entry into a totally different world of values and vision than that of their indigenous cultural world. The Church of today still follows the model narrated in the gospels: 'Jesus calls to conversion. This call is an essential part of the proclamation of the kingdom . . . In the Church's preaching this call is addressed first to those who do not yet know Christ and his Gospel. Also, Baptism is the principal place for the first and fundamental conversion' (1427). The Word of God confronts the actual life and world of the catechumen over an extended period of time.

The Word of God is not to be equated with teaching or preaching *about* Christ. As Vatican II reminded us, the Word of God is the presence of God. The Catechism takes the same perspective: 'To catechize is "to reveal in the Person of Christ the whole of God's eternal design reaching fulfilment in that Person" . . . Catechesis aims at putting "people . . . in communion . . . with Jesus Christ . . ." ' (426) and 'it is Christ alone who teaches . . .' (427). The catechumenal process implements these convictions by evangelizing within the context of prayer, self-examination and rituals of purification (such as exorcisms, blessings and anointings). Since the Word of God nourishes the whole person, catechumenal teaching 'while presenting Catholic teaching in its entirety also enlightens faith, directs the heart toward God, fosters participation in the liturgy, inspires apostolic activity, and nurtures a life completely in accord with the spirit of Christ'.[23] In brief, the sacraments of initiation are given to adults only when they have first heard the Word of God and begun to respond to it in faith and a life transformed by conversion (1229).

But such worship is a prayer that is shared with a community of witness to the crucified and risen Christ. There is no liturgy without Church.

Shared praise and ecclesial presence

As troublesome as some of Paul's Christian communities could be, he would never think of praising and thanking God without those communities. In fact, what is particularly striking in Paul's letters is the mixture of liturgical references and ecclesial reprimand – 'Because the loaf of bread is one, we, many though we are, are one body, for we all partake of the one loaf . . . You cannot drink the cup of the Lord and the cup of demons' (1 Cor 10:17, 21). How do our ideas of worship and Church connect with one another?

In an early section of the Catechism, the word 'Church' designates not only the local and the universal community of believers but also the liturgical assembly (752, with several Pauline citations for the latter designation). The Church is indeed a gathering of believers united in their praise and thanks to God. Later, the Catechism gives the derivation of the word 'liturgy'as a public work or a service performed 'in the name of/on behalf of the people' and then defines the Christian understanding of the word as 'participation of the People of God in the "work of God" ' (1069). Finally, one more definition of liturgy is given: 'an "action" of *the whole Christ (Christus totus)*' (1136). What is common to all these definitions is the conviction that worship profoundly and redemptively unites and dignifies people as God's own. Since contemporary Christian communities are as flawed as they were in Paul's day, this is an astounding definition of liturgy. Many Christians still think of the Church in purely institutional terms and of liturgy in largely ritual terms. To appreciate the accuracy of these definitions, we must examine the traditions behind them.

The Catechism, echoing Vatican II, cites one of the oldest of these traditions: 'For it was from the side of Christ as he slept the sleep of death upon the cross that there came forth "the wondrous sacrament of the whole Church" ' (1067). The biblical image of Eve drawn from the side of Adam is an obvious reference which the early Christian writers insightfully adapted to their teaching on the Church. The Genesis image implies the intimate connection between Adam and Eve, and its patristic adaptation has a similar purpose: to show the unity of Christ and his Church. Vatican II in its decree on the Liturgy provides an overview of the redemptive 'work' of God and of Christ so that the 'work' of the Church will be better understood. This 'work' is the mission to proclaim and celebrate the good news of our salvation: 'But the work they [the apostles] preached they were also to bring into effect through the sacrifice and the sacraments, the centre of the whole liturgical life.'[24]

When the Church, therefore, is called a 'sacrament', two ideas are offered us: first, the profound unity of Christ with the worship and work of the Church; second, the Church is best understood when it offers praise and thanks to God. This is further emphasized when the Council speaks of the different presences of Christ (in the eucharistic sacrifice and its minister, in all the sacraments and prayer of the Church as well as in his Word). The presence of Christ 'shines forth' in the praying Church: 'the Church is the Lord's beloved Bride who calls to him and through him offers worship to the eternal Father . . . no other action of the Church can equal its effectiveness by the same title and to the same degree'.[25] This last statement might be considered a pious exaggeration by some were it not for its reiteration shortly after in the same document: 'the liturgy is the summit toward which the activity of the Church is directed; at the same time it is the fount from which all the Church's power flows'.[26] In brief, there is no better way to describe the Church than in its worship, for there it also shows forth the saving work of Christ.

The Church that prays, works

Self-serving definitions of the Church and its liturgy seem to allow some Christians to be excused from taking part in the mission of the Church. The Catechism counteracts any such false attitudes: 'It is this mystery of Christ that the Church proclaims and celebrates in her liturgy so that the faithful may live from it and bear witness to it in the world' (1068). Here is the vital connection between liturgy and life: authentic worship enables us to live a gospel life and empowers us to give an effective witness to our world. Once again, the Catechism cites Vatican II as its authority for this statement where it is expressed even more strongly: liturgy enables ordinary Christians to 'manifest to others the mystery of Christ and the real nature of the true Church' (1068, citing the Constitution on the Liturgy 2). These are powerful assertions.

The instinctive response to such statements might well be: If this is so, why does there seem to be so little commitment and yet so much worship and sacrament in the Church these days?[27] If catechesis is to shape the lives of contemporary Christians, then it must be concerned with such a question. Although this problem will be addressed more thoroughly in Chapter 4, some initial response to this perennial problem is demanded here. Worship and sacrament can be used perversely to escape the presence of God as well as authentically to enter into that presence. The Church has traditionally discussed these possibilities under the heading of 'intention', that is, our reasons for doing an action.

Paul gives us an authentic reason for praising and thanking God, by examining the reason or intention Christ had in dying for us: 'He died for all so that those who lived might live no longer for themselves, but for him who for their sakes died and was raised up' (2 Cor 5:15). Paul links the paschal mystery of Christ's dying and rising (the basis of all liturgy, as we have seen) with the self-gift of Christians. With Christ's death, what had been impossible became possible – Christian selflessness that characterized the life and death of Christ. All witness is premised on this possibility of imitating Christ in a credible way. Any authentic intention in praising God is also tied to this possibility. When this Pauline reminder has been forgotten, the worship of the Church has become privatized and devotionalized beyond recognition, as the apostle's warning to his Corinthian community testifies: 'He who eats and drinks without recognizing the body, eats and drinks judgment to himself' (1 Cor 11:29).[28]

The Church as communion

Even when people understand why Church and liturgy are so closely tied together, they often do not see why the test of that connection is 'communion'. Before defining the term, we should recall some biblical data. First, recall a basic Pauline axiom: sin is division, redemption is unity. Second, the Church as 'the sacrament of Christ' shows forth this redemptive reconciliation and healing by a new and more profound oneness with God and one another. Paul forcefully reminds the Ephesians of these truths:

> But now in Christ Jesus you who once were far off have been brought near through the blood of Christ. It is he who is our peace, and who made the two of us one by breaking down the barrier of hostility that kept us apart ... reconciling both of us to God in one body through the cross, which put that emnity to death. (Eph 2:13–14, 16)

Finally, both Church and liturgy proclaim the coming reign of God that is characterized by perfect unity between God and all creation. Once more, the Catechism captures this idea succinctly: 'As the work of Christ liturgy is also an action of his Church. It makes the Church present and manifests her as the visible sign of communion in Christ between God and men' (1071). The Catechism describes the Church as 'communion' in several places (946, 1325). The Church as 'communion' might be defined as God's reconciled people gathered as a prophetic community to witness to the healing power of Christ's dying and rising and to the coming unity in the reign of God.[29] Like Christ, the Church must keep her eyes fixed on that perfect Future that God alone can promise, and she must shape her mission to the world from that vision. (In the next chapter we will see how the Holy Spirit effects this communion.)

The importance of this notion of 'communion' for the contemporary world can hardly be overemphasized. Social commentators regularly point to the anonymity (another form of division), alienation and greed that our First World cultures encourage. These divisive trends have become socially acceptable and culturally common in segments of our society. Consumerism, for example, is a 'respectable' form of divisiveness that separates those who can from those who cannot afford some of 'the better things' of life. In the audiovisual world of young people, lyrics of popular rock groups can preach an irresponsible sexuality that is predatory and selfish, another form of divisiveness. How can people hear of, much less believe in, the promised unity and communion of the reign of God in such a world if they do not see and experience a credible, if not perfect, symbol of that unity?

The Church must be that symbol of unity in this world. The Catechism connects Church, liturgy, and unity in this way: 'As the work of Christ liturgy is also an action of his Church. It makes the Church present and manifests her as the visible sign of the communion in Christ between God and men. It engages the faithful in the new life of the community and involves the "conscious, active and fruitful participation" of everyone' (1071). (The word 'participation', originally a Pauline term, has a long and rich history which we will discuss in Chapter 4.) For the moment, two practical implications of 'communion' given by the Catechism deserve our attention.

The first corollary of communion is that liturgy, like communion, is never a private affair (1140). It is the Church as 'the sacrament of unity' that celebrates liturgy, even though individuals have their own roles to perform (lector, minister of the eucharist, choir member and so on). This particular reminder is not meant simply to discourage liturgical rituals performed 'by an individual and quasi-privately' (1140) but to underline the attitude with which we should celebrate with one another. Liturgy asks more of us, as participants, than mere toleration of others in our vicinity or a grudging acknowledgement of them at the sign of peace. Such celebrations invite us to welcome and appropriate the belief that 'it is thus the whole assembly that is *leitourgos*, each according to his function, but in the "unity of the Spirit" who acts in all' (1144).

In religious education and homilies, it is of little use to speak of the Church as 'communion' and 'the body of Christ' if we do not invite people to re-examine their attitudes about the others with whom they worship and share a common hope. Being a member of the body of Christ is more than simply being a 'fellow worshipper' taking up adjacent pew space. The Catechism, in fact, offers a model for our ecclesial attitudes when it recalls that ' "sacraments make the Church", since they manifest and communicate to men, above all in the Eucharist, the mystery of communion with the God who is love, One in three persons' (1118). In other words, in each sacramental action we come into contact with the reality of the Trinity's own rich inner life. Participation in this reality is not a private possession but one that also enables us to see and welcome God in others.[30]

The second practical implication of communion is found in this same theme of the Church as communion, using the specific sacrament of the eucharist: 'In Baptism we have been called to form but one body. The Eucharist fulfills this call ...' (1396). Since Vatican II, most participants at Mass receive the eucharist. The Catechism reminds these participants that the eucharist 'is the efficacious sign and sublime cause of that communion in the divine life and that unity of the People of God by which the Church is kept in being' (1325). Again, it is Paul's teaching that validates this reminder: because we eat the one bread, we, though many, are one body (1 Cor 10:17).

Paul is speaking of more than institutional unity. He is referring to a communion of Christ and his people that announces God's perfect community at the end of time. The practical corollary is that the eucharist enables flawed people like ourselves to be in communion with one another because God is in communion with us. As noted above, one of St Augustine's recurring themes in his preaching about the eucharist reflects this same conviction: Body of Christ, be what you see, receive what you are.[31] Communication and communion not only have the same root in our language, they are both parts of the same reality that the eucharist proclaims and makes present: 'The faithful (*sancti*) are fed by Christ's holy body and blood (*sancta*) to grow into communion of the Holy Spirit (*koinōnia*) and to communicate it to the world' (948). In other words, no Christian community that has been fed with the sacraments can say that communion within and witness outside the Church are an impossible ideal.

Some conclusions

The Catechism presents a challenging mosaic to describe liturgy. In effect, this is not a mosaic of unrealizable ideals that are only to be proposed to and believed by naïve children or inexperienced catechumens. These dimensions of liturgy proclaim what God has done and is doing in our midst. They suggest a praying Church that must therefore be a witnessing Church. If we truly believe these classical descriptions of liturgy, then our excuses for vapid ceremonies as substitutes for authentic worship have been summarily dismissed.

On the other hand, the Catechism's understanding of liturgy also assumes that experiences of a saving God and a local committed Church are not alien to anyone who has worshipped in a Sunday eucharist or a weekend celebration of Christian marriage. No Christian, no matter how imperfect she or her local Church may be, has been deprived of such experiences. The paschal mystery which is at the heart of the liturgy has touched and healed many generations of flawed Christians like ourselves.

We have spoken a great deal of the Holy Trinity and of communion in this chapter. These themes have, in turn, dictated that of the next chapter, for 'communion with the Holy Trinity and fraternal communion are inseparably the fruit of the Spirit in the liturgy' (1108).''

Notes

1 The seminal article of L. Lies, 'Trinitätsvergessenheit gegenwärtiger Sakramententheologie', *Zeitschrift für katholische Theologie* 105 (1983), 415–29, calling for a stronger Trinitarian dimension to liturgical theology, influenced a number of other theologians, notably E. Kilmartin, *Christian Liturgy*, vol. I: *Theology* (Kansas City: Sheed & Ward, 1988), pp. 100–79.

2 The Catechism makes a distinction between 'theology', God's life within the Trinity, and the 'economy', God's works in creation and salvation (236).

3 For a similar statement in the Catechism, see 234.

4 C. LaCugna, 'The doctrine of the Trinity' in *Commentary on the Catechism of the Catholic Church*, ed. M. J. Walsh (London: Geoffrey Chapman, 1994), pp. 66–80, here p. 67.

5 C. LaCugna, *God for Us: The Trinity and Christian Life* (San Francisco: HarperCollins, 1991), p. 113. She also notes that such texts as Ephesians 1:3–14 and John 17, while not expressly mentioning the Trinity, suggest the saving plan of the Trinity and our participation in it (ibid., p. 130).

6 Ibid., pp. 112–13.

7 See LaCugna's remarks on the baptismal formula in Matthew: ibid., pp. 113–14.

8 For an English translation, see L. Deiss, *The Springtime of the Liturgy* (Collegeville, MN: The Liturgical Press, 1979), pp. 74–7.

9 'The term "child" as applied to Jesus in the earliest Christian texts is associated with this entire range of history and theology': ibid., p. 75, n. 3.

10 This axiom in no way contradicts the notion of the 'missions' of persons of the Trinity. See LaCugna, *God for Us*, p. 70.

11 Hippolytus, *The Apostolic Tradition* in the translation in Deiss, *The Springtime of the Liturgy*, p. 130.

12 H. Denzinger and A. Schönmetzer, *Enchiridion Symbolorum* (Freiburg: Herder, 1976), nos 1525–1526.

13 See J. A. Bernsten, 'Christian affections and the catechumenate', *Worship* 52 (1978), pp. 194–210.

14 Ambrose, *De Sacramentis* II, 21–22. The Latin and French texts from which I translated are given in *Des Sacrements, Des Mystères, Explication du*

Symbole, ed. B. Botte (Sources Chrétiennes 25bis; Paris: Cerf, 1959), pp. 86–7.

15 E. Mazza, *Mystagogy: A Theology of Liturgy in the Patristic Age* (New York: Pueblo, 1989).

16 Ibid., p. 130.

17 See the discussion in H. Conzelmann, *I Corinthians* (Philadelphia: Fortress), 1975, pp. 98–9.

18 Melito of Sardis, *Homily on the Pasch*: translation as given in Deiss, *The Springtime of the Liturgy*, p. 100.

19 For a classic commentary on this hymn, see G. Bornkamm, 'On understanding the Christ-Hymn (Phil. 2:6–11)' in *Early Christian Experience* (New York: Harper & Row, 1969), pp. 112–22.

20 J. D. G. Dunn, *The Theology of Paul's Letter to the Galatians* (Cambridge: Cambridge University Press, 1993), p. 120.

21 See the particularly fine commentary of C. K. Barrett on these verses in *The Second Epistle to the Corinthians* (London: A. & C. Black/New York: Harper & Row, 1973), pp. 168–70.

22 Paul VI, *On Evangelization* (*Evangelii Nuntiandi*) 18 (1975).

23 RCIA, 88: *Rite of Christian Initiation of Adults* (Chicago: Liturgy Training Publications, 1988), p. 38. The rite makes a distinction between instructional classes and celebrations of the Word, even though they may be connected. The rite gives four purposes to these celebrations: 'implanting in their hearts the teaching they are receiving ... instruction and experience in the ways of prayer ... explain to them the signs, celebrations, and seasons of the liturgy ... prepare them gradually to enter the worship assembly of the entire community': ibid., 82 (p. 40). The Catechism gives a more succinct description of the proclamation of the Word (1236).

24 Vatican II, *Sacrosanctum Concilium* (Constitution on the Sacred Liturgy) 6.

25 Ibid., 7.

26 Ibid., 10. In the preceding paragraph the Council noted that the liturgy presupposes a call to conversion and faith.

27 I have tried to deal with this specific question: R. Duffy, *Real Presence: Worship, Sacraments and Commitment* (San Francisco: Harper & Row, 1982).

28 In this text, 'recognizing the body' is key to its understanding. For all the possibilities, see C. K. Barrett, *The First Epistle to the Corinthians* (London: A. & C. Black, 1968), pp. 273–5 and for an ecclesial understanding of the phrase, see Conzelmann, *I Corinthians*, p. 202.

29 To appreciate the richness and importance of the Church as 'communion' the work of J.-M. Tillard is particularly helpful. See J.-M. Tillard, *Church of Churches: The Ecclesiology of Communion* (Collegeville, MN:

Liturgical Press, 1992) and *Chair de l'Eglise, Chair du Christ* (Paris: Cerf, 1992).

30 See also Catechism 815, where among the visible bonds of communion 'common celebration of divine worship, especially of the sacraments' is noted.

31 Augustine, *Sermon* 227 is but one example. The Catechism cites another famous example, *Sermon* 272 (1396).

3

Sacraments of the Spirit

ONE OF THE significant strengths of the Catechism is the acknowledgement of the role of the Holy Spirit in the celebration and theology of the liturgy. This emphasis accurately reflects developments in liturgical and sacramental theology in the past three decades as well as being a potentially creative opening in the area of ecumenical dialogues on sacramental questions. These trends, moreover, are based on a classical approach to all liturgical action: nothing is sanctified without the Holy Spirit (Cyril of Jerusalem). Boris Bobrinskoy mirrors this same tradition when he says that the Holy Spirit is 'the great choreographer of the ecclesial sacraments. In him and by him the encounter and union with Christ Jesus is realized.'[1] The context for this tradition is emphasized in two ways in the Catechism.

First, the connection of pneumatology (the theology of the Holy Spirit) and liturgy is announced unexpectedly in an earlier section of the Catechism, the commentary on 'I believe in the Holy Spirit' in the Creed. The opening lines contain two Pauline quotations (1 Cor 12:3; Gal 4:6) that are generally considered to have liturgical connections (683).[2] This sets the tone for a central idea in the Catechism: 'to be in touch with Christ, we must first have been touched by the Holy Spirit' (683), followed by a citation from Irenaeus on the action of the Holy Spirit in baptism. In other words, the *lex orandi* (the law of worship) is indeed supplying the inspiration for the *lex credendi* (the law of belief). As we will note later on, this approach should serve as a model for catechetics in general.

Second, the joint role of Christ and the Holy Spirit in our redemption is a constant theme. (This is in marked contrast to pre-conciliar theology texts which isolated the discussion of the work of the Holy Spirit from that of Christ.[3]) Once again, the Catechism gives a classical axiom: 'it is Christ who is seen, the visible image of the invisible God, but it is the Spirit who reveals him' (689).

The primary scriptural symbol of this joint role is not an external 'anointing' of Jesus by the Spirit but rather, 'the Spirit is his anointing' (690). This anointing occurs in 'the fullness of time' and the Catechism in a fairly thorough fashion details an intervening period when 'God's Spirit prepares for the time of the Messiah' (702). In creation, the covenant promises, the gift of the Law of God, and the exile of God's people, the action of the Holy Spirit is recalled (703–710). But it is in the section on the prophetic expectation of the Messiah, that the role of the Holy Spirit in preparing the People of the 'poor' (the humble and open people who await God's justice) is described as the greatest achievement of its hidden mission (716). Finally, the gospels highlight the action of the Spirit in the lives of John the Baptist, Mary and Jesus himself as he is anointed to proclaim the year of the Lord's favour.

A well-chosen quotation from Gregory of Nyssa in *On the Holy Spirit* explains the theological significance of such anointing: 'The notion of anointing suggests ... that there is no distance between the Son and the Spirit ... That is why the confession of the Son's Lordship is made in the Holy Spirit by those who receive him, the Spirit coming from all sides to those who approach the Son in faith' (690). The Catechism then describes the joint mission of Son and Spirit as the sending of the Holy Spirit by the glorified Jesus to unite us with him.

These same ideas are later repeated and expanded to make the connection with the Church: '... the mission of Christ and the Spirit becomes the mission of the Church ...' (730).

Pentecost is the moment in which the Spirit is given and the Holy Trinity is revealed. Once again the Byzantine liturgy for Pentecost captures the significance of this Pentecostal outpouring for the Church: 'We have seen the true Light, we have received the heavenly Spirit, we have found the true faith: we adore the indivisible Trinity, who has saved us' (732). Since the Spirit brings God's love and the consequent forgiveness of sins as well as the possibility of bearing fruit of the Spirit, the possibility of flawed people becoming the body of Christ is realized (734–736). As the Spirit anointed Christ, so she anoints the Church to be the sacrament of the mission of Christ and his Spirit (737–738).

While all this might seem to be a digression from our topic, the Catechism itself reminds us that it is not. Pentecost continues as 'through the Church's sacraments, Christ communicates his Holy and sanctifying Spirit to the members of his Body' (739), the same Spirit who is 'the artisan of God's works ... the master of prayer' (741). The working out of these insights in the worship of the Church will be a major concern later in this chapter, for they should supply an answer to the question: How does the Holy Spirit link creation and the new creation in Christ? This question, in turn, is crucial for a theology of worship.

A theology that insists on this joint role of the Son and Spirit in our redemption is usually described as a 'pneumatic Christology'. More important than the term, however, is the theological method it provides for doing a rich and pastoral liturgical theology, as we shall see. For the moment, it is enough to recall another beautiful summary of this joint redemptive role of Christ and the Spirit by Gregory of Nazianzus: 'Christ comes to the world, he [the Holy Spirit] precedes him; Christ is baptized, he gives testimony; Christ is tempted, he leads him (into Galilee); Christ accomplishes miracles, he accompanies him; Christ leaves, the Spirit succeeds him.'[4]

These introductory remarks summarize some of the Catechism's earlier sections on the Spirit in its discussion of the Creed. We will then turn to the later sections on the liturgy (with reference to sections on the sacraments). These sections answer two other crucial questions for our formation in worship: Why can we 'remember' and 'bless' God only by the power of the Spirit? How does the work of the Spirit transform our understanding of how worship and sacraments anoint us for the mission of the Church?

The Spirit over the waters

One of the attractions of Christian liturgy, even for some 'non-believers', is the way in which visible creation and its cultures are creatively used to praise God. Not only water, wine, and oil, but words and gestures form part of this visibility. The Catechism acknowledges this: 'A sacramental celebration is woven from signs and symbols. In keeping with the divine pedagogy of salvation, their meaning is rooted in the work of creation and in human culture ...' (1145). The instructions of the great catechumenal teachers, like Ambrose and Cyril of Jerusalem, employ this principle. The Catechism also insists on our human need to 'see' God's unseen reality and to hear God's voice through visible signs and symbols (1146–1148).

Yet sometimes in the history of theology, creation has been treated as one of God's regrets. To the extent creation is not valued, however, our new creation in Christ will inevitably seem less than it should. Heresies which have mistrusted creation have usually ended up losing their sense of the Uncreated. In ecumenical dialogues on liturgical and sacramental questions, this same suspicion occasionally appears. The Catechism offers a corrective to such disembodied theologies by linking the Holy Spirit and the work of creation and our new creation in Christ.

Once again, the Catechism establishes the religious nature of all creation by citing the liturgy. The text deserves to be quoted in full:

> It belongs to the Holy Spirit to rule, sanctify and animate creation, for he is God, consubstantial with the Father and the Son ... Power over life pertains to the Spirit, for being God he

preserves creation in the Father through the Son. (Byzantine Liturgy, 703)

Only to the extent that we value creation as God's gift can we then revalue the profound transformation that God's new creation effects. (St Francis of Assisi's *Canticle of Creation* is a lyrical expression of how both creations are connected.) With the Reformation polemics of the sixteenth century, this theology of creation was either neglected to some extent or even denigrated by some. The Catechism strongly reasserts the connection between the two creations:

> From the beginning until the end of time the whole of God's work is a *blessing*. From the liturgical poem of the first creation to the canticles of the heavenly Jerusalem, the inspired authors proclaim the plan of salvation as one vast divine blessing. (1079)

Both the celebration and the theology of liturgy rely on a dialectic of creation and new creation. And when a theology of new creation seems unreal, often enough it is because an authentic theology of creation is absent.

The Catechism provides an important corollary to this theology of creation from Irenaeus: God has so fashioned the human person that what is visible might show forth the divine (704). Although Augustine, Bonaventure or Thomas Aquinas might equally have been cited to make this classical point, the quote from the second-century Irenaeus reminds us that this theology of a creation overshadowed by the Spirit has a long history.

While this principle might seem to need no further emphasis, a closer look at our contemporary world might suggest otherwise. Those of us who have the privilege to teach and preach the faith must constantly remind ourselves of the cultural world of our students and listeners. Culture, after all, initially gives us our 'eyes' and 'ears' to view our world. Two examples of the impact of culture might prompt the reader to think of other such examples.

The first example is the environment. In our 'throw-away' societies there is regular disregard for and sometimes destruction of areas of creation (water, air, forests, wildlife, ecosystems, etc.) as if humans had created this gift of God. Certain forms of degrading poverty in our world can engender an irresponsible or pessimistic attitude toward the use of creation (useless destruction, drugs, disregard of the most basic health safeguards, etc.).

A second example is the attitude toward sexuality and the human body. Irresponsible sexual attitudes and behaviour, pornography, abortion and a rampant prurience are but symptoms of a deeper problem – a profound loss of awareness that God is creator. The importance of retrieving the role of the Holy Spirit in 'renewing the face of the earth' can hardly be exaggerated in our day.

How new is the new creation?

The liturgy's first gift to the Church is not ideas about God's action in our lives but the actualization of that action in our current situation, the recall of such actions in our past, and a privileged position from which to bless, acknowledge and thank God for all these actions. Liturgy deals with the actuality of our lives that have been and are constantly touched by God. This traditional teaching cannot be repeated too often, for it is so easy to go through the motions of liturgy (ritual words and actions) and confuse them with the appropriated meaning of liturgy.

When Paul speaks of Christians as a 'new creation' (2 Cor 5:17), he is speaking of what has been and is happening in our lives through the paschal mystery. Although 'new creation' sounds rather bland in English, Paul's Greek gives a very different impression. In effect, Paul characterizes this transformation in us as so radical that we are truly new people.[5] It is this unearned gift that is the source of our praise and thanks to God. When we recount how God has achieved such a transformation within the specific context of our own lives, narrative will not do. The liturgy provides two complementary actions to acknowledge this transformation: we 'remember' (Hebrew *zakar*) so that we can 'bless' (Hebrew *berek*). The cause of blessing is God's saving presence. These three terms ('remember', 'bless', and 'presence') deserve some explanation.

Blessing has a long history in the scriptures: 'From the beginning until the end of time the whole of God's work is a *blessing*. From the liturgical poem of the first creation to the canticles of the heavenly Jerusalem, the inspired authors proclaim the plan of salvation as one vast divine blessing' (1079). The Catechism then quickly surveys the Hebrew scriptures to give examples of its thesis (1080–1081). Since 'blessing' in ordinary experience might be understood as polite well-wishing or an innocuous ritual, a few remarks on the scriptural meaning of the term might be helpful.

Although there is disagreement among biblical scholars about some of the details of this form of prayer (e.g, its evolving private and liturgical use over the centuries), the prayer, in its early forms at least, was improvised, beginning with the formula 'Blessed be God' followed by the specific events in one's life that occasioned the prayer. The term *berakah* in Hebrew means not only to bless but also to thank and to acknowledge all that God has done in the individual's life. So, as the Catechism notes, from God's side blessing is word (the Latin and Greek root of 'blessing' means 'to speak well of') and gift, and from our side it 'means [man's] adoration, and surrender to his Creator in thanksgiving' (1078).

The Catechism begins its discussion of 'The Liturgy – Work of the Holy Trinity' by citing a *berakah* in the beginning of Ephesians and then commenting on it.

> Blessed be the God and Father of our Lord Jesus Christ, who has blessed us in Christ with every spiritual blessing in the heavenly places, even as he chose us in him before the foundation of the world, that we should be holy and blameless before him. He destined us before him in love to be his sons through Jesus Christ, according to the purpose of his will, to the praise of his glorious grace which he freely bestowed on us in the Beloved. (1077, citing Eph 1:3–6)

Notice, first of all, that the prayer is inspired by the fact of God redeeming us. (Even the tense of the Greek verbs 'blessed', 'chose', and 'destined' used in Ephesians indicate an action fully completed.) Although there is a general reference to redemption in the prayer, each person and community could give specific examples of this redemption in their own case. Second, our situation is totally changed, for we are now God's children. Third, the paschal mystery is always in the background, for the Pauline writer always has in mind a crucified Christ who was raised by God because he was obedient.

What better form of prayer for early Christians who enthusiastically welcomed the liberation from darkness that the paschal mystery had effected in their lives. This form of prayer had permeated the Temple and domestic prayer of Jesus' time. In the Last Supper accounts, Jesus is described as 'blessing' the bread and 'giving thanks' over the cup (Mark 14:22–23). Both terms seem to refer to the *berakoth* or blessings that marked the Passover meal as well as any sacred meal.[6] The earliest eucharistic prayers of New Testament communities no doubt employed this or related forms of improvised praise and thanks as did the extant first eucharistic prayers. The Catechism cites the second-century account that Justin Martyr gives of a typical eucharistic celebration in Rome: 'He [who presides] takes them [bread, and wine mixed with water] and offers praise and glory to the Father of the universe, through the name of the Son and of the Holy Spirit ... that we have been judged worthy of these gifts' (1345).

The Catechism retains its pastoral tone in presenting these ideas since it is the Church of today that must worship in spirit and truth. Liturgy is a powerful lens through which we see all that God has done for us in Christ and through the Spirit and experience that redemptive presence: 'In the Church's liturgy the divine blessing is fully revealed and communicated' (1082). Expressed differently, liturgy not only teaches us the mystery of salvation, it brings us in contact with that mystery. To appreciate the importance of this unique power of the liturgy, we must briefly look at the related ideas of 'remembrance' and 'presence'.

When memory is presence

A common feature of eucharistic prayers is that they 'recall' the events of Christ's life and death in a way similar to the Passover recollection of the saving events in Israel's history. The Catechism at this point (1084–1090) follows the same path. It reminds us that the saving mystery of Christ's history (his life, death, resurrection, his place at the right hand of the Father, his sending of the Spirit) is now present to us through the liturgy and the sacraments: 'By the action of Christ and the power of the Holy Spirit they [the sacraments] make present efficaciously the grace that they signify' (1084). Since the notion of 'presence' means much less in current popular usage than it does in the Judaeo-Christian tradition, a brief comment on its meaning and connection with 'remembrance' might be helpful.

In English 'to remember' always refers to the past. The Hebrew word *zakar* sometimes means 'to remember' in this sense, that is, to recall historically an event. But even an English translation of the Hebrew scriptures might suggest that there is another meaning for *zakar*. When Israel, for example, is so often told to 'call to mind what the Lord your God did to the Pharaoh and to all Egypt' (Deut 7:18), something other than an historical reminiscence is being demanded, since such recollections of themselves would have no redemptive value. Scripture scholars have pointed out, however, that God's call 'to remember' (*zakar*) can also mean to participate in a saving event that God actualizes in the present.[7] But what God does and what God is are not separate realities. Israel 'remembers' so that God's presence can evoke her response in presence. 'Presence', as used here, means taking what we are at a particular moment of our lives and offering it to another. In this sense, presence is much more than mere attention to another or the impact we have on others. Presence is the free gift of ourselves to God and to others in response to the God who is always present to us.

The Catechism has the same perspective when speaking of how God's saving presence touches us through the mystery of Christ's death and resurrection:

> His Paschal mystery is a real event that occurred in our history, but it is unique: all other historical events happen once, and then they pass away, swallowed up in the past. The Paschal mystery of Christ, by contrast, cannot remain only in the past ... The event of the Cross and Resurrection *abides* and draws everything toward life. (1085)

These lines contain a wonderful corrective for people who think of liturgy and sacraments as a sort of religious newsreel that reviews edifying events of the past. God's saving presence and action are at the heart of all authentic worship. The Catechism repeats the teaching of Vatican II that Christ is present in the Church and her liturgical celebrations of prayer, Word and sacraments, especially in the eucharist (1088).

These ideas can be somewhat lost because the Latin text of the eucharistic prayers and its translations employ the word 'memorial' to render the Greek term *anamnēsis* ('remembering'). The term 'memorial' in English refers to a past event commemorated in the present. But our discussion of *zakar* has also pointed to the meaning of actualization, the past made present in a real way, as an integral element of liturgical remembering. The Catechism, aware of the difficulty, notes that the eucharist is not merely a recollection but a proclamation of these saving events 'become in a certain way present and real' (1363). In an earlier discussion, our text employed the evocative phrase 'the "today" of her [the Church's] liturgy' (1095) to express this actualization of God's saving power in the liturgy.

The Church, as Justin Martyr's second-century narrative testifies, pastorally implemented all these insights long before there was a theology of 'remembrance', 'blessing', and 'presence'. In outlining the content of the eucharistic *anaphora* or prayer, the Catechism notes that 'In the *preface*, the Church gives thanks to the Father, through Christ, in the Holy Spirit, for all his works: creation, redemption and sanctification ... In the *anamnēsis* ... the Church calls to mind the Passion, Resurrection and glorious return of Christ Jesus ...' (1352, 1354). Later, in summing up the major themes of the entire prayer, 'the whole of creation loved by God' (1359) and 'gratitude for all his benefits ... accomplished through creation, redemption and sanctification' (1360) are given as the reasons for our thanksgiving and blessing.

The Catechism necessarily speaks of our praise and thanks to God in broad theological terms. People, however, have experienced the reasons for their particular *berakah* within the cultural and personal contexts of their own lives. Specific parishes have their own history of God's care and love. A sound catechetical approach will encourage communities and individuals to 'recall' in the two meanings of the Hebrew *zakar*: to remember how God has touched their past so that they may be present to God and others. This remembering and presence is possible because of the work of the Spirit in the assembled community and its worship.

The ongoing Pentecost

Theology does not so much propose theories about God's saving action as articulate what God has been and actually is doing. If this is forgotten, our preaching and teaching can be frustrating because they might seem to be speaking of the ideal and not the real world. The Catechism goes to the heart of the matter by insisting on the active role of the Holy Spirit in the midst of the Church's worship: 'In the liturgy the Holy Spirit is teacher of the faith of the People of God and artisan of "God's masterpieces", the sacraments of the new covenant' (1091). All our excuses for irrelevant and inauthentic liturgies are seriously challenged by this belief: the Spirit enables us to offer honest praise and thanks to God.

How does the Catechism go about explaining the Spirit's role in the worship of the Church? Our text leads us through four stages: the Spirit prepares us for the reception of Christ (1093–1098), recalls the mystery of Christ (1099–1103), makes present that mystery (1104–1107), and brings us into communion with Christ and thus, with one another (1108–1109). If examined more closely, the four stages actually seem to be a programme for a disparate group of people becoming the People of God and the Body of Christ. And so they are, for we cannot talk of worship and sacrament without talking about the Church within which liturgy is always celebrated. The Catechism indicates how such a worshipping community comes about: 'When the Spirit encounters in us the response of faith which he has aroused in us, he brings about genuine co-operation. Through it, the liturgy becomes the common work of the Holy Spirit and the Church' (1091). This Spirited encounter makes possible the ongoing Pentecost of the Church.

What would it mean to say that the Spirit prepares us for the reception of Christ? First of all, the Spirit reveals the mystery of Christ hidden in the Hebrew scriptures. This hidden mystery is called 'typological' because of the 'figures', or types, 'which announce him in the deeds, words and symbols of the first covenant' (1094). After the Easter events, the early Church could not read the psalms, the prophets, Passover and many other parts of the Hebrew scriptures without recognizing how God had prepared for the coming of Christ. (The example of typology most familiar to Christians is probably 1 Corinthians 10, where Paul treats the events of the Exodus as prefiguring the Christian sacraments.)

The preaching of the early Church found inspiration in seeing Christ within this context of the older scriptures, and the New Testament certainly mirrors that inspiration. In this typological rereading, as the Catechism notes, the flood and Noah's ark prefigure baptism, and manna in the desert pointed to the eucharist as 'bread from heaven' (1094). The Catechism's claim is, of course, verified in Luke's Emmaus account where the risen Christ, in response to the disillusionment of the two disciples, shows them how the message of

Moses and the prophets referred to the saving events of his death and resurrection: 'he interpreted for them every passage of Scripture that referred to him' (Luke 24:27).[8]

The catechumenal teachers also relied heavily on this approach. Ambrose, for example, tells his hearers that the column of light that led Moses and his people in the desert is 'Christ the Lord who has chased away the darkness of unbelief and has spread in human hearts the light of his truth and grace'.[9] As one writer observes, Ambrose's interpretation of figures (such as the column of light in our example) 'reveals a liberating presence of God, a presence that is mysterious but nonetheless real enough to play a determining role in a history'.[10]

It is important to remember, however, that these catechumenal talks explained a liturgical celebration and its symbols that the candidates had already experienced. These talks were pastorally designed to help the initiated enter more fully into the mystery of salvation and to draw out the moral implications of these liturgical experiences for their daily living. Ambrose, Cyril of Jerusalem and other such pastoral leaders never talked to their hearers as if they had no experience of this mystery (a point that preachers and catechetical teachers might learn from). Their explanations led the hearer to a more profound appropriation of symbol and its many layers of meaning and implications.

The Catechism obviously gives some importance to this notion of typology. This emphasis has, in turn, occasioned a good deal of discussion.[11] Among the problems with typology are the temptation to allegorize, to distort or miss the original meaning of the Hebrew scriptures, and even to adopt the anti-Semitic attitudes evident in some of these catechumenal leaders.[12] (The Catechism does attend to the potential anti-Semitic implications of typology in 1096 by pointing out the shared scriptural and liturgical heritage of the two traditions.)

The best response to these legitimate concerns is to observe how well the symbolic unfolding of the liturgy provides a context for commenting on and understanding the continuity of salvation history, and also an incentive for paying greater attention to the literal meaning of scripture (rather than immediately moralizing on a text as if that exhausted the meaning). The celebration of the Easter Vigil illustrates this point. In this celebration the proclaimed Old Testament passages on fire and water are not only dramatized but symbolically clarified by the liturgical actions done with the water and fire. At the heart of these symbolic actions is the work of the Holy Spirit who 'seeks to awaken faith, conversion of heart and adherence to the Father's will. These dispositions are the precondition both for the reception of other graces conferred in the celebration itself and for the fruits of new life which the celebration is intended to produce afterwards' (1098).

A universal catechism cannot be expected to explain in any detail how this typology within a symbolic context should be catechetically applied and liturgically indigenized for a local Church. Perhaps a remark of Ambrose might suggest a clue. Ambrose's explanation of why the Church at Milan performed the washing of feet in the initiation rites and the Church of Rome did not is usually taken only as an indication that local Churches may have differing customs while maintaining a collegial uniformity.[13] But his explanation that God has gifted all of us with reason is in fact a catechetical as well as liturgical reminder to the local Church. The sociocultural meaning (and, therefore, a source for the symbolic meaning) of water and fire even in English-speaking countries is not as uniform as catechetical approaches might sometimes suggest. The symbolic reluctance of some congregations at the Easter Vigil to be even in physical proximity to symbolic actions of seeing fire and feeling water is paralleled by recitations rather than proclamation of the scriptural meaning of these events. Within a specific culture, then, liturgical symbols as well as scriptural images must be explained with a keen eye on cultural understandings.

What does human reason tell us in our local situation? It tells us, as it told Ambrose, that both our culture and our worship converge by the power of the Spirit to enable a local

Church to appropriate God's redemptive meaning: 'every liturgical action, especially the celebration of the Eucharist and the sacraments, is an encounter between Christ and the Church ... The preparation of hearts is the joint work of the Holy Spirit and the assembly, especially of its ministers' (1097, 1098).

Calling the Spirit

One of the most valued 'rediscoveries' of Western theology in this century is the role of the Holy Spirit in the liturgical life of the Church. The Holy Spirit, of course, was always mentioned in theological texts as having a role in the sacramental life of the Church, but until the post-conciliar reform of the Roman Canon it would have been difficult to find the *epiclesis* (i.e., the prayer calling down the Holy Spirit on the eucharistic gifts to sanctify them) in the eucharistic celebration.[14] In other words, there seemed to be no 'law of worship' that would substantiate and clarify the 'law of belief', in this case, the task of the Spirit in making Christ present, for example, in the eucharist. The theologies of the West emphasized almost exclusively the words of institution over the bread and wine as making Christ present.

The Eastern Church, however, had never lost its awareness of the crucial role of the Spirit in the prayer and worship of the Church. Cyril of Jerusalem's explanation to the newly baptized of how Christ becomes present in the eucharistic celebration is typical of this theology: '... we pray the loving God to send the Holy Spirit over the gifts laid here to make the bread the body of Christ, and the wine the blood of Christ; *for all that the Holy Spirit touches becomes sanctified and transformed'.*[15] The italicized words of the quotation reflect the crucial role attributed to the Holy Spirit in liturgical action. The Catechism acknowledges the traditional emphases of the Churches of the East and West: 'The Church Fathers strongly affirmed the faith of the Church in the efficacy of the Word of Christ and of the action of the Holy Spirit to bring about this conversion [of the bread and wine]' (1375).

The Catechism's teaching on the Spirit has been enriched by the restored epiclesis in all the post-conciliar eucharistic prayers of the Roman Catholic Church, since 'the law of belief' is always enriched by the 'law of worship'.[16] The sections on the work of the Holy Spirit in recalling and making present the mystery of Christ (1099–1107) accurately mirror the importance of this topic in liturgical theology and practice. In effect, these sections might be understood as a commentary on Paul's reminder to the Christians at Rome that Christian worship would be impossible were it not for the pleading of the Spirit in their behalf (Rom 8:26-27).[17]

When the Catechism calls the Spirit 'the Church's living memory' (1099), the text reflects our previous discussion of *zakar*, an actualization of God's saving acts. The two areas where this 'recalling' is exemplified are the liturgical proclamation of the Word of God and the anamnesis in the eucharist. First, our text emphasizes the importance of the liturgical readings of scripture and the homily since the Spirit 'enlivens' that Word for us so that we can live out its meaning (1101). Second, the Spirit then enables the listeners to respond in 'consent and commitment' (1102). Third, this enabling action of the Spirit helps the liturgical assembly be 'a communion in faith' (1102).

The teaching of the Catechism on these last points is particularly important when the Sunday liturgy of the eucharist strikes some people as a combination of mostly incomprehensible readings and irrelevant homilies to be endured rather than be enriched by.[18] Often enough the experience of some younger people in religious education classes and theology courses is no better.[19] This does not always reflect religious indifference but rather a real thirst for God's word that nourishes their daily living. The insistence of our text, therefore, on the role of the Spirit in the preaching and teaching of God's word should raise certain questions.

Do those who teach and preach God's word have enough respect for the action of the Holy Spirit in the lives of their listeners? If God has not been absent from the daily lives of people, then their religious experience must be addressed.

The Word of God is proclaimed so that Christians may understand not only what God asks of them but what God has already done for them so that they might respond. Christ certainly could not be accused of 'neglecting doctrine' in his talk to the disciples on their way to Emmaus, but their reaction should be our guide: 'Were not our hearts burning inside us as he talked to us on the road and explained the scriptures to us?' (Luke 24:32).

This same emphasis on the role of the Spirit in 'recalling' and actualizing these saving events of God (1104) continues in the epiclesis, which is 'the heart of each sacramental celebration' along with the anamnesis (1106). Since the 'Spirit of communion' (1108) is called down upon the eucharistic community so that it may indeed be the body of Christ, much more may and should be expected of that community. The Catechism speaks of three pastorally practical results of the Spirit's descent on the assembled community: a presence that bespeaks a Christ 'for others', eager for unity, and ready to take part in the mission of witness and service (1109).

The epiclesis in other sacramental actions should also be noted. The Spirit is called over the water so that those baptized may be born of water and the Spirit (1238), and over the chrism of Confirmation for the sealing of the Spirit (1297, 1300), over the sick by praying 'in the faith of the Church' (1519), in marriage over the couple as 'the communion of love of Christ and the Church' (1624), and so on.

Finally, the Catechism points to the Holy Spirit as our teacher of eschatology, that is, the one 'who hastens the coming of the kingdom ... he causes us really to anticipate the fullness of communion with the Holy Trinity' (1107) by his transforming power in all liturgical celebration. The reign of God may seem very vague and utopian to some but it is the heart of the gospel message that Jesus preached. The importance of this teaching cannot be overemphasized. In effect, we are being reminded that God through the Spirit is always doing more than we might realize – opening our lives to God's Future that even now is touching the present.

Some concluding remarks

In one of its summary paragraphs, the Catechism reminds us:

> The mission of the Holy Spirit in the liturgy of the Church is to prepare the assembly to encounter Christ; to recall and manifest Christ to the faith of the assembly; to make the saving work of Christ present and active by his transforming power; and to make the gift of communion bear fruit in the Church. (1112)

If the results of the liturgy celebrated in a Christian community seem meagre at times, then a selective response to the Spirit's action may be the problem. The saving presence of Christ that the Spirit effects in the liturgy is there for personal but not privatized reception. That same presence enables a parish or religious community to long for that gift of communion to 'bear fruit in the Church' (1112). The same Spirit anoints them as it did Christ for the sake of the world's salvation.

The discussion of the Spirit in this chapter leads to another topic in the Catechism's treatment of liturgy: faith-filled and fruitful participation in word and sacrament. This theme will be the focus of the next chapter.

Notes

1 B. Bobrinskoy, *Communion du Saint-Esprit* (Begrolles-en-Mauges, France: Abbaye de Bellefontaine, 1992), p. 45.

2 For 1 Cor 12:3 see H. Conzelmann, *I Corinthians* (Philadelphia: Fortress, 1975), p. 206. Galatians 4:6 is often considered an example of ecstatic speech, which I would think of as usually occurring in a liturgical setting. See J. D. G. Dunn, *Jesus and the Spirit* (Philadelphia: Westminster, 1975), pp. 240–2.

3 This approach is summarized by E. Kilmartin: '... the work of sanctification of humanity is conceived as the work of the Triune God in an undifferentiated way. It is attributed to the Spirit, but only in terms of "appropriation", namely, because the Spirit signifies divine life. It is not predicated of the Spirit because of the personal mission by which the Spirit exercises a personal role in the economy of salvation ...': *Christian Liturgy*, vol. I: *Theology* (Kansas City: Sheed & Ward, 1988), p. 108.

4 Gregory of Nazianzus, *Discourse on the Holy Spirit* XXXI, 29: as cited by Bobrinskoy, *Communion du Saint-Esprit*, p. 65.

5 J. Ysebaert, *Greek Baptismal Terminology* (Nijmegen: Dekker & Van der Vegt, 1962), pp. 89–90, 131–5. Also, J. Behn, 'Kainos' in *Theological Dictionary of the New Testament*, vol. III (Grand Rapids, MI: Eerdmans, 1965), pp. 447–50.

6 See A. Bouley, *From Freedom to Formula* (Washington, DC: The Catholic University Press, 1981), pp. 17–31; C. Di Sante, *Jewish Prayer: The Origins of Christian Liturgy* (New York: Paulist Press, 1991), pp. 141–71. There is a debate over whether another form of praise associated with sacrifice (*todah*) rather than *berakah* might be the model for early eucharists. In either case, the Catechism's explanation is still both correct and helpful. For an excellent summary of the debate as well as an analysis of these early eucharistic prayers, see D. N. Power, *The Eucharistic Mystery* (New York: Crossroad, 1992), pp. 55–7, 83–6, 91–4.

7 See B. S. Childs, *Memory and Tradition in Israel* (London: SCM Press, 1962), pp. 51–3.

8 'This is the Lucan way of casting the OT data; it is his global christological use of the OT ... Luke has his own way of reading the OT and here puts it on the lips of Christ himself ... Such a reading of the OT explains what Luke meant when in the prologue of the Gospel he spoke of "the events that have come to fulfillment among us" (1:1)': J. Fitzmyer, *The Gospel According to Luke (X–XXIV)* (New York: Doubleday, 1985), p. 1558.

9 Ambrose of Milan, *On the Sacraments* III:22: *Des Sacrements*, ed. B. Botte (Sources Chrétiennes 25bis; Paris: Cerf, 1959) pp. 72–3.

10 E. Mazza, *Mystagogy: A Theology of Liturgy in the Patristic Age* (New York: Pueblo, 1989), p. 16. Mazza gives a very useful description of all of Ambrose's vocabulary of biblical typology and says that the latter's meanings for 'figure' and 'type' are, for all practical purposes, identical: ibid., p. 21.

11 For an overview of this discussion see C. Dooley, 'Liturgical catechesis according to the Catechism' in *Introducing the Catechism of the Catholic Church: Traditional Themes and Contemporary Issues*, ed. B. Marthaler (New York: Paulist Press, 1994), pp. 87–98, here pp. 90–5.

12 Mazza's frequently cited observation is: 'Allegory is the death of mystagogy' (ibid., p. 13). See his discussion of this problem of allegory and typology: ibid., pp. 9–13.

13 Ambrose of Milan, *On the Sacraments* III, 5: *Des Sacrements*, pp. 94–5.

14 For a discussion of lack of an epiclesis in the Roman Canon, see J. Jungmann, *The Mass of the Roman Rite*, vol. II (New York: Benziger Brothers, 1955), pp. 187–94.

15 Cyril of Jerusalem, *Mystagogical Catechesis* V, 7:*Catéchèses Mystagogiques,* ed. A. Piédagnel (Sources Chrétiennes 126bis; Paris: Cerf, 1988), pp. 154–5, my emphasis.

16 The way in which the epiclesis was restored is problematic. Since the Western Church at a certain point began to emphasize the words of institution as consecratory, a 'split' epiclesis was used in the restoration so as to avoid any suggestion that the epiclesis was consecratory. Thus, the first epiclesis before the consecration asks the Holy Spirit to sanctify the gifts while the second epiclesis after the consecration is over the community. The Eastern Church has usually regarded the epiclesis as consecratory while not excluding the importance of the words of institution. See A. Kavanagh, 'Thoughts on the new Eucharistic Prayers' in *Living Bread, Saving Cup,* ed. K. Seasoltz (Collegeville, MN: Liturgical Press, 1982), p. 109; B. Bobrinskoy, *Communion du Saint-Esprit,* pp. 264–9; E. Kilmartin, 'The active role of Christ and the Holy Spirit in the sanctification of the eucharistic elements', *Theological Studies* 45 (1984), pp. 225–53.

17 For a particularly eloquent commentary, see E. Käsemann, *Perspectives on Paul* (Philadelphia: Fortress, 1971), pp. 127–37.

18 For the homiletic situation in the United States, see A. Greeley, *The Catholic Myth: The Behavior and Beliefs of American Catholics* (New York: C. Scribner's, 1990), pp. 148–53.

19 See P. H. McNamara, *Conscience First, Tradition Second: A Study of Young American Catholics* (Albany: State University of New York, 1992).

4

Nourishing faith and sacrament

THE HISTORY OF sacraments is both fascinating and complex because sacramental theory and practice do not always seem to agree. This statement might appear to contradict an axiom that the Catechism has cited several times: 'the law of worship establishes the law of belief'. The axiom is true if 'law of worship' is understood, first of all, to mean what God does so that we can both worship and understand in spirit and truth. But what St Thomas Aquinas and St Bonaventure were teaching on the sacraments in the University of Paris was not necessarily what was actually happening in the parishes of medieval Europe. In other words, theory does not always reflect or challenge liturgical practice.

The sections of the Catechism on the sacraments do not have the same 'tone' as those on the liturgy, perhaps because they take their inspiration more from the theory of sacraments than from the practice of liturgy. The corrective, however, is supplied by our text. The sections on the sacraments should be read within the context of the liturgical sections of the Catechism since sacraments are part of the liturgy. The liturgical sections attempt to articulate how God enables us to pray as a community.

In an early section of 'The Paschal Mystery in the Church's Sacraments' (1114–1121), several general but important concerns are briefly explained since they apply in various ways to all seven sacraments. In one sense, these concerns have already been discussed in the previous liturgical sections. But they take on a more specific character in this section. 'Sacraments' is a more limited term than 'liturgy'. Liturgy includes all the public prayer and worship of the Church (thus, the office of the hours is liturgy) while sacraments are limited to seven specific liturgical expressions linked to distinct roles and tasks within the Church.

Whose sacraments are they?

The importance of visibility in symbol was mentioned in an earlier chapter. The gospels detail Christ's visible actions as well as his spoken words since they complement one another (recall Christ making mud with his spittle to apply to the eyes of the blind man and then telling him to wash it away). The Catechism regards these actions and words as anticipations of the paschal mystery (1115), that is, God's saving acts attuned to our created nature. We need signs and symbols that are seen, touched, and heard in order to understand and respond on all the levels of our being. The Catechism cites the insightful phrase of Leo the Great: 'what was visible in our Saviour has passed over into his mysteries' (1115).

Since the Catechism has already insisted in several places on the ecclesial context of liturgy, it is not surprising that it defines 'sacrament' within that same context. Sacraments are, first of all, described as 'powers' coming from the Body of Christ (1116). To understand what 'powers' are being referred to, the reader must check the Lucan citations that the text gives (Luke 5:17; 6:19; 8:46) to explain the term. In all three episodes, Jesus' power is that of healing (in contrast to other scenes in which his power is for exorcizing or calming the forces of nature). The tradition of understanding sacraments as the healing power of God is very old. It is reflected in the patristic and medieval medical synonym for sacraments: *medicamenta*, 'medicines'.

This description, in turn, derives from the very early title of Jesus as the *medicus* (doctor). In the gospels (e.g., Mark 2:17; Matt 9:12–13; Luke 5:31–32), in response to criticisms of his proclaiming forgiveness of sins as he heals, Jesus reminds his hearers that it is the sick who need a doctor. Early Christian writers extend this image to the sacraments. Origen, for example, says:

> So much for ordinary physicians. Now look at Jesus the heavenly physician. Come inside his room of healing, the church. Here comes a woman unclean from childbirth, a leper expelled from the camp due to his unclean disease; and because this Jesus the physician is also the Word of God, he applies, not the juices of herbs, but the sacraments of the Word to their diseases.[1]

Origen closely associates the Church with the doctor Christ and, therefore, with his medicines, the sacraments.

In explaining the connection between Church and liturgy in Chapter 2, we suggested an axiom 'The Church that prays, works'. In other words, you cannot separate the praise and thanksgiving of the community for the gift of salvation from the mission of that community – to announce that same good news to others. Therefore, the sacraments do not afford a privatized healing that is unconnected with the gospel mission. We are healed so that we may be healing. The Catechism's next description of sacraments as 'actions of the Holy Spirit at work in his Body, the Church' (1116) should certainly be understood in this same way. When we examined, in the previous chapter, the joint role of Christ and the Spirit in the work of our redemption, the link between our anointing by the Spirit and that of Christ was made clear: we 'put on Christ' to the extent that we are, like him, 'on account of others'. We are not sanctified apart from the work of the gospel which, in turn, is enabled by the work of the Holy Spirit within the assembled and praying Church.

This rich biblical manner of defining the sacraments is in marked contrast to the pre-conciliar method of describing them in terms of 'matter and form' (a philosophical theory applied with some ingenuity and varying success by medieval theologians to the description of sacraments). The Catechism points to the mandate of the Church to discern which liturgical celebrations should be called sacraments and cites similar discernment in regard to the recognition of the canon of the scriptures and to the doctrine of faith (1117).

Historically this sacramental discernment was demonstrated in the gradual recognition of seven sacraments by the Church. The reader will remember that up to the twelfth century the number of the sacraments was still debated with estimates ranging up to the teens. Some connection between a sacrament and Christ (for its institution) was obviously necessary. While it seemed that there was such an institution for baptism and eucharist, it was more difficult to link other sacraments with Christ's direct institution.[2] (Distinctions were made between major and minor sacraments or between direct and indirect institution of the sacraments.[3]) The major point of this section of the Catechism is that in the Church's gradual recognition of seven sacraments the prophetic and healing work of Christ is continued, and the sacraments are empowered in a way similar to Christ's ministry of healing.

These connections are further emphasized when the Catechism explains the phrase 'sacraments *of the Church*' by noting that they are 'by her' and 'for her' (1118). Once the Church is recognized as the real symbol of Christ's work as animated in her by the Holy Spirit, then that symbol also communicates to the world the presence of a saving and loving God. This is a favourite theme in the writings of Augustine: 'And Adam slept when Eve was created from his side. Adam is the figure of Christ, Eve the figure of the Church. Hence she is called the mother of the living. When was Eve created? While Adam slept. When do the sacraments of the Church flow from the side of Christ? When he sleeps on the cross.'[4]

In many different ways Augustine returns to the same point: in observing the Church as she prays, celebrates the sacraments, and preaches the gospel, it is the union and communion of the assembly that speaks to the world as God sanctifies its members. The *Catechism* sums up this conviction in speaking of the eucharist as 'the efficacious sign and sublime cause of that communion in the divine life and that unity of the People of God by which the Church is kept in being' (1325).

Servant among servants

Three decades after Vatican II it is not surprising to hear the Church described as a 'priestly community'. After all, Pius XII had insisted on this biblical teaching (1 Peter 2:5) in his encyclical on the Mystical Body in 1943, and seven centuries earlier Thomas Aquinas had pointed to initiation and its 'character' as enabling Christians to take part in the liturgy of the Church. The Catechism repeats this same teaching: Baptism and confirmation make us part of the priesthood of all the faithful and enable us to celebrate the liturgy (1119, 1268, 1546). The sacrament of orders enables those called to perform specific roles in the Church 'in the name of Christ' (1119) and 'guarantees that it really is Christ who acts in the sacraments through the Holy Spirit for the Church' (1120). The ministerial or ordained priesthood is called to serve the baptismal priesthood (1120).

From this distinction, the Catechism then explains the statement of Vatican II that these two priesthoods, while ordered to one another, are essentially different: all Christians in living a life of faith, hope, and charity exercise their priesthood while the ordained ministries help all the baptized to fulfil their priesthood (1547). In brief, not everyone can do everything in the Church on the basis of their initiation. The unrepeatable sacraments of baptism, confirmation, and orders confer a 'character' by which all share in Christ's priesthood though given different roles (1121).

There are no surprises here. The one point that might disconcert some is found at the end of 1120: 'The ordained minister is the sacramental bond that ties the liturgical action to what the apostles said and did, and through them, to the words and actions of Christ, the source and foundation of the sacraments.' The purpose of the statement is a legitimate concern to connect the liturgical life of the Church with Christ. This same concern is also expressed when the Catechism repeats the classical phrase that the priest acts in *persona Christi capitis* ('in the person of Christ the head') (1548).

The legitimate concerns about rooting the Church's ministry in that of Christ and in asserting how the Church discerns
the specific roles of those unordained and ordained should
be enriched by the theological scholarship on the subject.
Nor should the considerable biblical and historical research
of the last decades on the origin and development of ministries in the Church be neglected.[5] This does not dismiss the
discussion on ordained ministries but it does nuance it.
Second, the Eastern Church has regularly spoken of the
priest acting *in persona ecclesiae* ('in the person of the
Church'). With this perspective the priest's action *in persona
Christi* has its ecclesial context as well as its christological
basis.[6] The role of the Holy Spirit is also retained in saying
that the priest acts in the person of the Church, and thus, of
Christ.[7] (The Catechism does acknowledge this ecclesial
dimension but only as a corollary to *in persona Christi*
(1552–1553).[8]) This ecclesial approach reminds all that ordination is not a private possession but one received for the
sake of the mission of the Church and service of all: 'This
priesthood is *ministerial*... The exercise of this authority must
therefore be measured against the model of Christ, who by
love made himself the least and the servant of all' (1551,
emphasis in the text).

The word from the cross

The faith demanded by Jesus in response to his good news is
a constant and challenging theme in the gospel accounts.
Paul continues that theme: 'But how shall they call on him in
whom they have not believed? And how shall they believe
unless they have heard of him? And how can they hear unless
there is someone to preach?' (Rom 10:14). Without this
connection, Paul's startling line about not having been sent
to baptize but to preach the gospel (1 Cor 1:17) is disconcert-
ing as is his summary of that gospel, 'the word of the cross' (1
Cor 1:18). Faith that comes from hearing of a crucified Lord
is the prelude to sacrament: '... the sacrament is prepared

for *by the word of God and by faith* which is assent to this word' (1122, emphasis in the text).

The connection between faith and sacrament might seem obvious, but reception of the sacraments without faith is not unknown. Louis Villette's two-volume *Foi et sacrement* ('Faith and Sacrament') summarizes the thought of all the great theologians of the Church on this connection.[9] Much of this thought was prompted as much by pastoral concern as it was by theological controversy. Pastors like Augustine were familiar with people in their community who received sacraments without an adequate faith or who deferred them because they did not want the moral consequences of such faith.

Augustine, however, is quite clear on how such ordinary elements as water can be used in sacraments: 'From whence does the water which touches the body and purifies the heart have such power except from the act of the word, *not because it is said but because it is believed.*'[10] It is with those same concerns that he said that '... even within the bosom of the Catholic church, we prefer the good catechumen to the bad baptized person'.[11] It should be added that Augustine, throughout his writings and in his homilies, stresses the importance of hearing the word of God so that faith might be deepened and, thus, the sacraments more fruitfully received.

In the history of sacraments, the word of God gradually became a difficult if not incomprehensible word, not only because it was no longer in the language of the people but because the preaching of that word left much to be desired. On the other hand, when gospel preaching flourished, then sacramental life was renewed. The fervent preaching, for example, of the mendicant orders (Franciscans, Dominicans, Servites, and others) in the thirteenth century had a powerful effect on the reception of the sacraments of the eucharist and of penance.[12] Vatican II, as cited by the Catechism, was keenly aware of the integral connection of word and sacrament: 'The People of God is formed into one ... by the Word of the living God ... the sacraments are sacraments of faith, drawing their origin and nourishment from the Word' (1122).

The Catechism in its discussion of the word of God in sacramental celebrations does briefly cite the current rituals but does not draw its inspiration from those sources. But it should be also noted that all the post-conciliar sacramental rituals have restored the celebration of the word of God as an important element. (The Council of Trent had called for this same reform without any success in the sixteenth century.) In speaking of the catechumenal process, for example, the Catechism notes that 'the *proclamation of the Word of God* enlightens the candidates and the assembly with the revealed truth, and elicits the response of faith, which is inseparable from Baptism' (1236, emphasis in the text). In the sacrament of penance and reconciliation the reading of the word of God is 'to illuminate the conscience and elicit contrition' (1480) while in the anointing of the sick 'the words of Christ, the witness of the apostles, awaken the faith of the sick person and of the community to ask the Lord for the strength of his Spirit' (1518).

Although the Catechism says comparatively little about how the word of God deepens faith and prepares the Christian for a fruitful reception of a sacrament, its importance should be obvious from the citations given. It also points to the evangelization that is sometimes necessary before a sacrament is received. Paul VI in his letter *On Evangelization* insisted on speaking of this task as an essential characteristic of the whole Church community: 'Those who have received the good news and who have been gathered by it into the community of salvation can and must communicate and spread it.' [13] Later in the same letter, in clarifying how the word of God should continue to energize the 'paschal church', Paul VI highlights the importance of the Sunday homily that is clear, relevant, and 'profoundly dependent on gospel teaching'.[14] Finally, proclaiming the word achieves its full efficacy when there is a 'permanent and unbroken intercommunication, between the word and the sacraments ... The role of evangelization is precisely to educate people in the faith in such a way as to lead each individual Christian to live the sacraments as true sacraments of faith – and not to receive them passively or to undergo them.'[15] We will return to this point in the next chapter in discussing how our intention to celebrate and worship honestly is shaped by the word of God.

The law of worship

The ancient axiom, 'the law of worship establishes the law of belief', has been mentioned several times. The Catechism teaches that in the celebration of the sacraments, the Church confesses the apostolic faith; it then goes on to say: 'the Church believes as she prays. Liturgy is a constitutive element of the holy and living Tradition' (1124). The axiom is first found in the writing of Prosper of Aquitaine, who argued for the need of God's unearned grace (the law of belief) by pointing to the general intercessions for the Good Friday liturgy (the law of worship).[16] Another historical example might clarify this axiom. During the fourth century, when the debates on the divinity of the Holy Spirit were causing much division, Basil argues from the liturgy: if the Spirit is worshipped with the Father and Son, then the Spirit must also be divine.[17]

The historical examples are clear enough, but is this axiom still a viable principle for theology today? The Catechism, for example, notes that the law of worship is 'one of the essential criteria of the dialogue that seeks to restore the unity of Christians' (1126). One avenue of dialogue proposed by some theologians, for example, since the late 1960s is the possible ecumenical implications of an epicletic prayer in the ordination rites of other Christian traditions.[18] Another example is the document *Baptism, Eucharist, Ministry* published in 1982 by the World Council of Churches, which then sent it to all the major Christian traditions throughout the world for their 'reception'.[19] This 'consensus' document does derive some of its statements from areas of convergent liturgical practice of the Churches. Over the last thirteen years more than 195 official responses of Churches have been received by the Council. The Roman Catholic response, for example, notes with approval the document's statement that 'it is through the *epiklesis* prayed for by the competent minister that the gift of the Spirit is conferred on the person ordained'.[20] Although Rome must then ask about the episcopal succession necessary for the 'competent minister', the liturgical practice of the epiclesis at the ordination of ministers in some of the Churches has provided an ecumenical opening that is important.

In the past two decades there has been a good deal of theological reflection on how this axiom about the link between worship and belief operates within the Catholic tradition.[21] In this discussion, there is a common concern that the worship of the Church again be a source of rich theological insight and that the insight gained might in turn challenge our worship to a more honest participation and reflection. As already noted, worship itself is a response to the word of God and its enabling call to faith. The axiom, then, about worship as a source of doctrine and theology is not simply the formula for an intellectual method of achieving new insights in theology, but a reminder about the divine origin of faith, sacrament, and theology. The Catechism, in repeating Vatican II's reminder that the purpose of sacrament is to sanctify, to build up the Body of Christ, and to give worship to God (1123), also provides the larger context for understanding the ultimate goals behind the axiom.

On the level of the local Church, the catechumenate once again provides a practical model for this process of moving from the experience of liturgical prayer and expression to a deepening awareness of what God teaches the assembled Church. The Rite of Christian Initiation of Adults directs that the catechesis is to be accommodated to the liturgical year, 'solidly supported by celebrations of the word ... This catechesis leads the catechumens not only to an appropriate acquaintance with dogmas and precepts but also to a profound sense of the mystery of salvation in which they desire to participate.'[22] Theologians like Augustine and Ambrose who

were both theologians and catechumenal leaders would recognize the familiar pastoral wisdom of this direction as part
of their own experience.

Current liturgies and future feasts

The final concerns of Chapter One of the section on 'The
Sacramental Economy' are taken up with two related issues:
the connection of sacraments to salvation (1127–1129) and
the final and unending liturgy (1130). The Catechism quotes
Thomas Aquinas' wonderful summary (though readers will
probably be more familiar with its paraphrase in the liturgy of
Corpus Christi): 'Therefore a sacrament is a sign that com-
memorates what precedes it – Christ's Passion; demonstrates
what is accomplished in us through Christ's Passion – grace;
and prefigures what that Passion pledges to us – future glory'
(1130; *Summa Theologiae* III, 60, 3).

The Catechism repeats a classic teaching: sacraments confer what they signify if we celebrate them 'worthily in faith'
(1127). Behind that straightforward sentence there is a rich
and complex history of sign and symbol. Augustine, as noted
earlier, showed the importance of proceeding from the
seen to the unseen in his sacramental teaching. Among his
several descriptions of a sacrament, his most familiar one
is 'the *visible* sign of invisible grace'. The Catechism also
follows this path: 'The sacraments are *perceptible* signs
(words and actions) accessible to our human nature' (1084,
1145–1152).

There are two important points to note about this process
of moving from the visible to the invisible. First, this sequence
is at the heart of symbolic thinking and action. Symbol
enables us to move from one level of thinking and acting to
another more profound level. ('Symbol', as used here, refers
to reality, not some shadow of it, as in popular speech when
someone says 'It's only symbolic'. The Catechism seems to
use 'sign' and 'symbol' as synonyms, e.g. 1145.) Thus, when
Augustine explains the phrase 'Body of Christ' said in giving
the eucharist to the newly initiated ('Be what you see, receive

what you are'), he also illustrates this symbolic thinking and action. The communicant moves from the visible sign of Christ's invisible eucharistic presence to another invisible reality linked to that sign, the ecclesial community as 'Body of Christ'. Second, on the catechetical and pastoral level, the importance of the words and actions of a sacramental event should be obvious in their celebration. (For instance, immersion in the waters of baptism, especially for adults, respects the visibility of the symbol more than sprinkling with water.)

The Catechism goes on to say that a sacrament does confer what it signifies (is efficacious) precisely because 'Christ himself is at work: it is he who baptizes ...' (1127). This explanation returns to a very old tradition. By the time Augustine was challenging the Donatists' position (that sacraments are only valid when the minister as well as the recipient of the sacrament are holy), the traditional position of the Church was that it was Christ who baptizes (1128). When a sacrament is celebrated according to the intention of the Church, then the power of Christ and the Spirit is the operative dynamic, not the holiness of the sacramental minister (1128).

The great medieval theologians were aware of this tradition, but symbolic thinking was no longer a part of most people's culture, and the importance of the Holy Spirit in sacramental celebrations had become less appreciated. The Catechism continues its explanation of why a sacrament 'works' by noting the power of the Spirit 'in the epiclesis of each sacrament' (1127). This remark brings us back to one of the most important insights of classical sacramental theology at the same time that it clears a major obstacle in our ecumenical dialogue with the Orthodox Church.

It might be very difficult for someone to accept the sacraments as 'necessary for salvation' of the believer (1129) if the whole paschal context of liturgy and sacrament were forgotten. Since the mystery of the death and resurrection of Christ is the basis for our salvation, and faith-filled sacramental participation brings us into that mystery, then it is not hard to understand why the Catechism speaks of the fruit of sacramental life as partaking in the divine life and union with Christ (1129). The Spirit enables us to be like Christ and be one with him.

In the previous chapter we discussed, in Pauline terms, sin as division and separation and salvation as union and communion. This salvation, of course, will only be realized fully in the reign of God. All liturgy looks toward that reign when (to use the beautiful image of the scriptures) we will sit at the feast of God in perfect communion. The Catechism, employing one of the earliest recorded liturgical prayers, speaks of that goal: *Marana tha,* 'Come, Lord Jesus!' (1130, citing 1 Cor 16:22). It is the liturgy that teaches Christians the theology of the reign or kingdom of God. It is the liturgy that teaches Christians how to long for that reign.

Our text shows us the model for looking forward to God's reign – Christ at the Last Supper. In Luke's account, Jesus, while urging his disciples to drink of the cup of wine, refuses to drink it until the reign of God is accomplished (Luke 22:15). Luke presumes that the reader knows some important background information. First, wine is one of the privileged symbols of the reign of God in the scriptures (e.g. Isa 25), an important part of the menu at God's unending feast. Wine must be drunk even by the poorest of Jews at the Passover meal because of this meaning. Second, there are instances of individuals and groups prophetically refusing to drink wine until the reign of God was accomplished (e.g., the Rechabites, John the Baptist).[23] Luke, then, seems to present the Last Supper as looking toward the unending feast, and to picture Jesus prophetically refusing the cup to remind those who partake of it that the final feast is not yet fully here.

Liturgy makes real the otherwise vague idea of 'heaven' by teaching us how to long for what we have only an inkling of – God's feast of victory and union. Paul is aware of this understanding of the eucharistic liturgy: 'Each time you eat this bread and drink this cup, you proclaim the death of the Lord until he comes' (1 Cor 11:26).

Some conclusions: of celebrants and celebrations

On closer reading, there is a surprisingly insistent pastoral dimension to these sections of the Catechism. The assembled Christian community is constantly reminded that its celebrant is the Lord himself and its liturgical animator is the Holy Spirit: 'the liturgy is the work of the whole Christ, head and body. Our high priest celebrates it unceasingly in the heavenly liturgy, with the holy Mother of God, the apostles, all the saints and the multitude of those who have already entered the kingdom' (1187). The entire Christian community is 'liturgist' according to the baptismal priesthood of all and the ordained ministry of some (1188). Above all, each celebration of 'today' is already a celebration of tomorrow: 'It is in this eternal liturgy that the Spirit and the Church enable us to participate whenever we celebrate the mystery of salvation in the sacraments' (1139). The possibility for authentic participation in the liturgy is founded on such reminders.

But if such participation is to achieve its full expression and to result in effective mission to the world, then another reminder of the Catechism is in order: 'liturgical celebration tends to express itself in the culture of the people where the Church finds herself . . . liturgy itself generates cultures and shapes them' (1207). The final chapter will examine these claims.

Notes

1 Origen, *Homily* 8 on Leviticus, as cited by A. von Harnack, *The Mission and Expansion of Christianity in the First Three Centuries*, English translation by J. Moffat (Gloucester, MA: Peter Smith, 1963), p. 110, n. 4. For further discussion see R. Duffy, *A Roman Catholic Theology of Pastoral Care* (Philadelphia: Fortress, 1983), pp. 42–7 and 'The Medicus tradition in early medieval sacramental theology' in *Festschrift for Aidan Kavanagh*, ed. N. Mitchell and J. Baldovin (Washington, DC: Pastoral Press, forthcoming).

2 The definitive work on institution and number of the sacraments in the crucial early scholastic period is W. Knoch, *Die Einsetzung der Sakramente durch Christus* (Münster: Aschendorff, 1983. For a concise history of the question, see A. Ganoczy, *An Introduction to Catholic Sacramental Theology* (New York: Paulist Press, 1984), pp. 43–54.

3 Recent scholarship would emphasize the influence of Pseudo-Dionysius' writings on the final numbering of the sacraments since 'seven' is considered a perfect number: see M. Seybold, 'Die Siebenzahl der Sakramente', *Münchener Theologische Zeitschrift* 27 (1976), pp. 113–38.

4 Augustine, *Enarrationes* on Psalm 40, 10 (CC 38, 456, 16–20), my translation.

5 In particular, see J. Colson, *Ministre de Jésus-Christ ou le Sacerdoce de l'Evangile* (Paris: Beauchesne, 1966); A. Lemaire, *Les Ministères aux origines de l'Eglise* (Paris: Cerf, 1971); also J. Delorme (ed.), *Le Ministère et les ministères selon le Nouveau Testament* (Paris: Seuil, 1974); P. Bernier, *Ministry in the Church: A Historical and Pastoral Approach* (Mystic, CT: Twenty-Third Publications, 1992).

6 See E. Kilmartin, 'Apostolic office: sacrament of Christ', *Theological Studies* 36 (1975), pp. 243–64; W. Kasper, 'Das Amtverständnis dispensiert nicht' in *Interkommunion in Diskussion und Praxis*, ed. A. Kirchgässner and H. Bühler (Düsseldorf: Patmos, 1971), pp. 109–10.

7 Once again, this is a major concern of the Eastern Churches: see the discussion in R. Hotz, *Sakramente – im Wechselspiel zwischen Ost und West* (Cologne: Benziger, 1979), pp. 235–41.

8 For a balanced discussion of this question, see P. Rosato, 'The sacrament of Orders' in *Commentary on the Catechism of the Catholic Church*, ed. M. J. Walsh (London: Geoffrey Chapman, 1994), pp. 303–17, here 311–12.

9 L. Villette, *Foi et sacrement* (2 vols; Paris: Bloud et Gay, 1959–64).

10 Augustine, *Tract on John* 80, 3, my emphasis. For a discussion of this text, see Villette, *Foi et sacrement*, vol. I, pp. 231–9; for the subsequent misunderstanding of the same text, see vol. II, pp. 258–62.

11 Augustine, *On Baptism* IV, 21, 28. For an older English translation, see *The Nicene and Post-Nicene Fathers*, vol. IV (Grand Rapids: Eerdmans, 1979), p. 460.

12 For a detailed history of the ministry of the word, see B. Cooke, *Ministry to Word and Sacraments* (Philadelphia: Fortress, 1976), pp. 219–340.

13 Paul VI, *On Evangelization* 13; English translation in *Proclaiming Justice and Peace: Documents from John XXIII to John Paul II*, ed. M. Walsh and B. Davies (Mystic, CT: Twenty-Third Publications, London: Collins, 1984) p. 210.

14 Ibid., 43: *Proclaiming Justice and Peace*, p. 220.

15 Ibid., 47.1: *Proclaiming Justice and Peace*, p. 222.

16 See P. de Clerck, 'Lex orandi lex credendi. Sens originel et avatars historiques d'un adage équivoque', *Questions Liturgiques* 59 (1978), pp. 193–212.

17 See C. LaCugna, 'Can liturgy ever again be a source for theology?', *Studia Liturgica* 19 (1989), pp. 1–16; and *God for Us: The Trinity and Christian Life* (San Francisco: HarperCollins, 1991), p. 118.

18 J.-M. Tillard, 'L'Eucharistie et le Saint-Esprit', *Nouvelle Revue Théologique* 90 (1968), pp. 363–87; P. Lebeau, 'Vatican II and the hope of an ecumenical eucharist', *One in Christ* 5 (1969), pp. 379–404.

19 *Baptism, Eucharist and Ministry* (Faith and Order Paper no. 111; Geneva: World Council of Churches, 1982).

20 M. Thurian (ed.), *Churches Respond to BEM*, vol. IV (Geneva: World Council of Churches, 1988), p. 34.

21 Among the more important contributions, see A. Kavanagh, *On Liturgical Theology* (New York: Pueblo, 1984), pp. 74–7; D. N. Power, 'Two expressions of faith: worship and theology', *Concilium* 82: *Liturgical Experience of Faith* (1973), pp. 95–103 (New York: Herder & Herder, 1973); G. Lukken, 'La liturgie comme lieu théologique irremplaçable', *Questions Liturgiques* 56 (1975), pp. 97–112.

22 Rite of Christian Initiation of Adults, 75.

23 See J. Jeremias, *The Eucharistic Words of Jesus* (3rd edn; London: SCM Press, 1966), pp. 51–3, 208–16; P. Lebeau, *Le Vin Nouveau du Royaume* (Paris: Desclée de Brouwer, 1966).

5
Future celebrations now

ALBUMS OF FAMILY photos allow us to glimpse the context of people's lives in a way that individual photos do not. The previous four chapters of this book have briefly sketched the profile of the Church from a number of angles. In the first chapter we discussed the ways in which the Church teaches and celebrates God's salvation and gives us a way of gospel living. Worship, it was suggested, teaches in ways that intellectual explanations cannot. The second chapter spoke of the sources of the Church's life, energy, and mission – the life of God and the paschal mystery. God's saving 'outreach' to us evokes our praise and thanks. The third chapter looked at the Holy Spirit as the animator of liturgy in its sacramental expressions of initiation, eucharist, and the other sacraments. Expressions such as 'remember', 'thanks and praise' and 'in the Spirit' point to the ways in which a community may constantly reassemble in closer unity and communion. The key topic of the fourth chapter was how sacramental participation can deepen our faith life. The word of God was viewed as a bridge to honest sacrament and to a more mature faith. The sum of these impressions is a family called to gospel commitment and unselfish worship for the sake of the salvation of the world.

This chapter comments on the final sections of 'The Sacramental Economy' in the Catechism (1136–1206). In each century since the time of Christ the Church has celebrated liturgy in a constantly changing world. The perennial wisdom and insight of her worship has deepened, but not changed in its gospel essentials. But the Christians of the First or Third Worlds at the end of the twentieth century do not inhabit the same historical or sociocultural world as that of Augustine's fifth-century North Africa or Thomas Aquinas' thirteenth-century Italy. Good celebrations of God's saving love are always a balance between the perennial values of effective liturgy and the special profile that an age and its culture bestow.

Participants or observers?

The Catechism in describing the heavenly liturgy as 'wholly communion and feast' (1136) is not about to excuse earthly liturgies from having similar qualities. The Catechism notes that the liturgy of the saints is 'without signs' (1136) because it intends to deal with our liturgies that are replete with signs. Above all, when our text states that our liturgies are a 'fore-taste of that heavenly liturgy' (1090), we can be sure that the demanding implications of that phrase will be detailed. In a very real sense, these sections draw out the pastoral corollaries for all the previous discussions of liturgy and sacrament.

It is not unusual in any discussion of worship to see some reference to the panoramic and dramatic descriptions of the heavenly liturgy in the book of Revelation that are read in the liturgy on the feast of All Saints and on a number of other occasions. What is striking in the Catechism's citation is the choice of images from the book of Revelation that point to the paschal mystery: 'It then shows the Lamb, "standing as though it had been slain"; Christ crucified and risen, the one high priest of the true sanctuary, the same one "who offers and is offered, who gives and is given" ' (1137, citing also St John Chrysostom's anaphora). In the same vein, Revelation's enumeration of the various participants in this heavenly liturgy fills out this picture of redemption finally accomplished and eternally praised.

But the Catechism by proceeding in this fashion has very quietly made two other important points that will then be developed. First, there are no private liturgies in the reign of God nor can there be in our earthly celebrations. Second, there is a statement of continuity of God's original intention of salvation and its final and irrevocable accomplishment. The line of liturgical participants reaches from the heavenly powers and the people of the Old and New Covenants even to the martyrs of the last times. The Church's teaching on the communion of saints not only reinforces the public character of her worship but is a witness to the profound religious as well as cultural awareness of the importance of continuity in families and its final goal.

To prevent any cynicism about the pastoral reality of all this, the Catechism points to the animating force of all authentic worship, the Holy Spirit: 'It is in this eternal liturgy that the Spirit and the Church enable us to participate whenever we celebrate the mystery of salvation in the sacraments' (1139). This reminder is both reassuring and challenging because it takes away some of our favourite excuses for liturgies that do not seem to speak of heavenly liturgies. But if God in the power of the Spirit (described by our text from Revelation as 'the river of the water of life ... flowing from the throne of God and of the Lamb' (1137) empowers such worship, what responsibilities does the liturgical community have?

Christians as celebrants

We have already discussed the Church as 'community' and 'communion' in previous chapters. The Catechism now expands that discussion: 'the whole assembly ... is *leitourgos*, each according to his function, but in the "unity of the Spirit" who acts in all' (1144). *Leitourgos* is a derivative of the same Greek root for 'liturgy' that we discussed earlier. It connotes someone who does a public work, that is, a work for the benefit of all. Vatican II's Constitution on the Sacred

Liturgy, cited at this point in the Catechism, insisted that liturgy is not a private function but 'celebrations of the Church which is "the sacrament of unity" ... Therefore, liturgical services pertain to the whole Body of the Church' (1140). In classical fashion, our text has gone to the heart of the matter in stating the attitude that the celebrating community and its individuals must have.

Like any good teacher, the Catechism does not assume that mention of the 'public' character of worship will be enough to change any privatized notions of worship that the reader might have. Therefore, it goes on to say that liturgical celebrations have two ecclesial characteristics: they 'manifest and have effects on' the Church (1140). But how does the liturgy, first of all, 'show forth' the Church?

The reader needs to recall earlier discussions on the nature of symbol and how it always leads to a deeper truth. The example of St Augustine's explanation of 'Body of Christ' not only illustrated this characteristic of symbol but also explains how a symbol 'manifests' the Church. Augustine shows the multivalent (or many-levelled) meaning of a familiar ritual phrase: 'Body of Christ' means both the eucharistic presence of Christ and the ecclesial presence of Christ, head and members. But if this were only an intriguing intellectual explanation, then Augustine could not reasonably say: '*Be* what you see, receive what you *are!*' He would be demanding more than we could realistically expect.

Symbol, however, enables as well as points out. Augustine's community by its participation in the eucharist has been empowered to 'show' the meaning of that body: the unity that salvation brings in Christ and now is visible in this community. This, after all, is also Paul's argument: we are one *because* we eat the one bread (1 Cor 10:17). Paul is pointing to the effect the liturgy of the eucharist has on the Corinthian community (being the Body of Christ) and why it can thus manifest the presence and meaning of that same Christ (the Corinthians are the Body of Christ).

Telltale signs of participation

The Catechism takes seriously both the beautiful descriptions of the Church as a 'spiritual house' and a 'holy priesthood' (1141) and its consequent responsibility of 'full, active, and conscious *participation* in liturgical celebrations' (1141, citing Vatican II). In English, 'participation' may be used in a weak sense, perhaps to describe only what a television audience might do. The Christian understanding of the word is much more dynamic: participation is the appropriation of the paschal mystery that we celebrate. In other words, we not only go through the rituals of commitment but we become more committed to God's values and goals as seen in the death and resurrection of Christ.

Paul uses both a Greek noun (*koinōnia*) and a verb (*metechein*) for this word several times in 1 Corinthians. It is also much used, in its Latin translation (*participatio*), in the homilies and theological writings of great pastors and teachers like Augustine and Leo the Great. In all these cases it invariably has something to do with worship. Therefore it should not be surprising how frequently it also appears in the older prayers of the Roman liturgy and in the documents of Vatican II.

As interesting as the history of the term 'participation' might be, our present concern is its practice: How do we appropriate what we celebrate? The answer involves our intentions. The word 'intention' comes from a Latin verb that means 'to stretch into'. The basic meaning of the word, then, indicates a stretching from where we are into a new position (much as runners do when they stretch). Intention implies a dynamic process in which we deepen the reasons and motivations for our actions and take more responsibility for them. We can perform the ritual of a kiss, but it is our intention that will transform that kiss into a symbol that both manifests and has an effect on our love.

Two other descriptions of intention might complete the picture. Asking God for the right intention is beautifully expressed in the Armenian liturgy when the celebrant as he bends over the altar prays 'Imprint on my heart, Lord, the posture of my body'. The American bishops expressed the same idea in describing authentic participation in worship: 'We are celebrating when we involve ourselves meaningfully in the thoughts, words, songs, and gestures of the worshipping community . . . when we mean the words and want to do what is done.'[1]

The purpose of our discussion so far has been to draw out some of the implications of the call of Vatican II and the Catechism for full, conscious and active participation. But after all, should not the intention of the Church suffice? It does for the valid celebration of a sacrament, but as Augustine constantly pointed out to the Donatists, it does not assure a fruitful celebration for participants unless they join their intention to that of Christ and his Church. Their intention is summed up in the meaning of Christ's death for the world and the effect it should have for us: Christ died for us so that we might no longer live for ourselves but for Christ (2 Cor 5:15).

To appreciate the importance of intention for participation in worship, the reader needs to recall that intention involves 'the *totality* of the person's orientation to the world at the time'.[2] Intention helps us confront the sometimes subtle gap between our daily lives and our Sunday worship. We symbolize our worship out of our lived experience that has been both formed and sometimes deformed by our intentions. The connection between intention and authentic liturgical participation has always commanded the pastoral attention of the great Christian teachers like Augustine. Like many other great theologians, Augustine wondered how Judas could have received the eucharist and then betrayed Christ. His answer, with its characteristic play on the words 'good' and 'bad', captures the problem of intention in liturgical participation: It is not because the bad one (Judas) received a bad thing (the eucharist) but because the bad one received a good thing (the eucharist) badly.[3] In other words, intention cannot destroy a symbol but it can distort our participation in that symbol.

A final word should be said about the cultural and ecclesial ways in which intentions are also shaped. Our culture in supplying us with a system of meanings and values also contributes to the ways in which we tend to construct our intentions. This is not restricted to purely 'secular' domains. A few examples from past and current cultures might clarify this point. Peter Brown, for example, in his studies of Christianity in the fourth and fifth centuries has demonstrated how Christians began to think of patron saints in similar ways to their cultural idea of a patron.[4] Within any contemporary culture, there are a number of expressed and unexpressed reasons for participating in seasonal or patriotic rituals, as well as certain sociocultural reasons for 'belonging' to a particular Christian tradition, that may have nothing to do with Christianity. Finally, since language itself is a cultural product, its use even in the translated ritual language of the Church has cultural overtones. We turn, then, to the question of inculturation in the liturgy.

The liturgy of the world

The Catechism has seven articles that deal with signs and symbols (1145–1152). We have already touched on some of the themes that these articles mention, those of creation (Chapter 1) and of symbols (Chapter 4). Our text speaks of sacramental celebrations '. . . woven from signs and symbols. In keeping with the divine pedagogy of salvation, their meaning is rooted in the work of creation and in human culture' (1145). The Catechism devotes four paragraphs (1146–1149) to some of the implications of creation and culture as a context for worship. Because the Catechism's discussion assumes a great deal of the reader, we will try to review at least some of the background of the question.

The liturgy has a wonderful way of summing up complex theological ideas in a concise form. The opening prayer for the First Sunday after Christmas, for example, says: 'Almighty God, you wonderfully created and yet more wonderfully restored the dignity of human nature. In your mercy, let us share the divine life of Jesus Christ, who came to share our humanity ...'. The prayer in a few words states the close connection between God's act of creation and of 'new creation' or salvation. As noted in Chapter 1, Paul's 'new creation' presumes a complete theology of creation. Out of all this, God will shape our redemption and we will proclaim our thanks.

To help focus the question more closely, the Catechism goes on to speak of one aspect of creation – the communication of spiritual reality through the physical reality of signs and symbols (1146). 'God speaks to man through the visible creation' (1147). Reminiscent of the creation psalms ('Sun and moon, stars and light, praise the Lord!') and the *Canticle of Creation* of St Francis of Assisi, our text notes that all aspects of creation point to God's greatness and nearness. Is there more to be said about this?

Karl Rahner toward the end of his life wrote a particularly beautiful essay 'On the theology of worship'.[5] His theme is summed up in his phrase 'the liturgy of the world'. He sees creation as a school in which we learn to welcome and respond to symbols of God's goodness that are etched in time and space. This world is the place of God's saving actions and thus, in Rahner's sense, the primary liturgy. But in looking at the contemporary world with its violence, exploitation, and environmental irresponsibility, he then asks whether people of today can indeed find and praise the God of creation.

Rahner's answer bears careful reading. God has created us with a capacity for the mystery of God. It is this symbolic capacity that enables us to find the 'traces of its Creator' (1147): 'these perceptible realities can become means of expressing the action of God who sanctifies men, and the action of men who offer worship to God' (1148). In realistic fashion, Rahner insists on our God-given ability, even in a created world flawed by our irresponsibility, not only to find God there but to employ creatively this creation in shaping our praise and thanks. Rahner sums up these connections between creation and new creation:

When we say that we celebrate the death of the Lord until he
returns, we are saying that we are giving space and time
explicitly in our own life to the cross of Jesus ... This ecclesial
worship is important and significant, not because something
happens in it that does not happen elsewhere, but because
there is present and explicit in it that which makes the world
important.[6]

Our culture gives us a particular way of looking at creation.
In the post-industrial First World, the very fact that environmental issues can provoke such anger and division on both
sides of the question should tell us that a theology of creation
should not be presumed. Christians who are comfortable
with the doctrine that 'God created all things' may not be
culturally willing to see all the implications of that doctrine.
In the national catechisms of our First World countries there
should be some attempt to deal with the specific cultural
attitudes that might prevent young people from seeing any
connection between their 'real' world and the God who
makes all things 'new' in Christ.

'Blessed are you for this bread and wine'

Symbols transform meaning. The gift of a rose on an anniver-
sary transforms the meaning of that gift into another
meaning, that of love, while not denying the first meaning,
the beauty of the flower. For Francis of Assisi all creation
spoke of the love of God and his crucified Son: 'Praised be
You, my Lord, with all your creatures, especially Sir Brother
Sun, Who is the day and gives us light. And he is beautiful and
radiant with great splendour; and bears a likeness of you,
Most High One.'[7] This is not simply an overwrought poetic
imagination at work. The Catechism reminds us that 'the
liturgy of the Church presupposes, integrates and sanctifies
elements from creation and human culture, conferring on them
the dignity of signs of grace, of the new creation in Jesus
Christ' (1149, my emphasis).

The Catechism rightly emphasizes the importance of the
signs of creation (candles, water, etc.), human life (washing,

anointing, etc.) and the history of salvation (the rites of Passover) in a liturgical celebration (1189). The Catechism has also acknowledged that these celebrations are expressive of the culture of the participants (1207). The problem is that a culture (e.g., that of the post-industrial countries) may devalue signs as well as value them. Water pollution, for example, is a growing problem today in many countries. The only potable water may be bottled.

This is not an insuperable obstacle to water's use as an evocative sign of the waters of baptism. But it does mean that the local Church should at least make as much effort as advertising agencies in finding new ways to revalue old signs. (Liturgists could learn something in this regard from the Evian and Perrier advertising.) The Catechism does not (and should not be expected to) suggest specific cultural contexts for these signs. Liturgists and other experts in the culture must be concerned with the cultural revaluing of these signs.

Something has already been said about the 'elements from creation' and how culture gives us a particular frame of reference for looking at that creation. In an earlier chapter, Paul VI's challenge to close the gap between culture and evangelization was noted. Now the Catechism deals with the question of inculturation, that is, how are elements with their cultural meanings integrated into worship with its meanings.

Liturgy with an accent

Although the Catechism first treats singing and music (1156–1158), holy images (1159–1162), liturgical time (1163–1178) and architecture (1179–1186), we need to postpone their discussion until the larger theme of inculturation (1200–1206) has been discussed. The Catechism had already mentioned this theme in an earlier section on the mission of the Church: 'It must involve a process of *inculturation* if the Gospel is to take flesh in each people's *culture*' (854, emphasis added). The terms inculturation and culture are labels for

entire disciplines. We need to define these terms before we
see how the Catechism comments on their connection with
liturgy.

One could do no better than to start with a classic definition of culture that Clifford Geertz gives: 'an historically
transmitted pattern of *meanings* embodied in *symbols*, a system
of inherited conceptions expressed in symbolic forms by
means of which people *communicate*, perpetuate and develop
their knowledge about and attitudes toward life'.[8] The italicized words should remind the reader of themes already
discussed in this book. Both liturgy and anthropology are
concerned with meanings about life and the world around us
that are communicated through symbols. These meanings
are never private because they have an impact on other
people as well as on ourselves. Perhaps Geertz had this in
mind when he remarked that culture is public because meaning is.[9]

When Geertz offers an anthropological description of religion, it is not surprising that it resembles his definition of
culture in some important ways. He speaks of religion in
terms of symbols and meaning that 'establish powerful, pervasive, and long-lasting moods and motivations' in people.[10]
These 'moods and motivations' resonate with the 'attitudes
toward life' of his earlier definition of culture and indicate
how religion involves the whole person's outlook, the affective as well as the intellectual dimensions. If we now examine
Vatican II's remarks on culture and inculturation, we will find
similar concerns voiced from a different perspective.

Vatican II's concern with culture sprang from its debates
on the problems of evangelization and inculturation. In its
Pastoral Constitution on the Church in the Modern World
(*Gaudium et Spes*), the Council had spoken of culture as a
collage of elements that make visible the complexity and the
values of human beings and their communities.[11] From its
long missionary experience, the Church had always been
aware, in varying degrees, of the importance of culture in
mediating the gospel to a particular people.[12] In line with the
theology of creation discussed earlier, the Council reminded

missionaries that the rich heritage of Christ was to be discovered in the culture.[13] For culture deals with the aftermath of creation. The process of evangelization should set up a dialogue with the host culture so that there could be transformation of all things in Christ.

This conciliar line of thinking was continued in Paul VI's writings on evangelization, as we have already seen. More recently John Paul II has been equally forceful on the subject: 'A faith which does not become culture is a faith which has not been fully received, not thoroughly thought through, not fully lived out.'[14]   So far, the importance of culture as a primary means of communication has been the subtext of these conciliar and papal writings. When we turn to the question of inculturation, we will once again find a discussion of symbol.

The Catechism links the themes of culture and inculturation:

> The celebration of the liturgy, therefore, should correspond to
> the genius and culture of the different peoples ... It is with
> and through their own human culture, assumed and
> transfigured by Christ, that the multitude of God's children
> has access to the Father, in order to glorify him in the one
> Spirit. (1204)

Anscar Chupungco, who has written extensively on inculturation, offers a definition that complements that of the Catechism. He describes it as a process in which the local Church absorbs and then employs the communication patterns (thought, language, ritual) of its culture in its worship.[15] In contrast to adaptation or juxtaposition of cultural elements in the liturgy, inculturation is a demanding pastoral and theological process of dialogue that recognizes key cultural symbols that resonate with liturgical symbols of praise and thanksgiving to God.[16]

Historically, local Churches have been engaged intermittently in this process throughout the centuries.[17] The Catechism justly notes that 'the mystery of Christ is so unfathomably rich that it cannot be exhausted by its expression in any single liturgical tradition' (1201) and lists some of those traditions (Roman, Ambrosian, Alexandrian, Armenian, etc.: 1203). This diversity is the result of the Church's mission to different peoples in different historical periods. Since culture connotes symbols that communicate key meanings of a particular group of people, it is not surprising that the local Church facilitates 'access to the Father' (cited above from 1204) by creatively employing its cultural 'language' of actions, images, thought patterns, and vocabulary.

The Catechism distinguishes what is immutable and changeable in the celebration of the liturgy (1205). The immutable in the liturgy is whatever is divinely instituted (such as the words of institution in the eucharist) while the Church can change other parts (e.g., the number or the language of the liturgical readings). The unity of these celebrations is guaranteed by adhering to what is truly immutable, and diversity is encouraged where the pastoral mission of the Church and the fruitful participation of Christians prompt it. There is also an understandable concern about the type of diversity that might cause division. This possibility can be prevented if there is 'fidelity to the common faith, to the sacramental signs that the Church has received from Christ, and to hierarchical communion' (1206).

The Catechism offers a final penetrating remark about inculturation that bears closer scrutiny: 'Cultural adaptation also requires a conversion of heart and even, where necessary, a breaking with ancestral customs incompatible with the Catholic faith' (1206). Creation belongs to God but it has been flawed by the presence of radical sin, that is, an environment that is hostile to the gospel message of redemption. Inculturation, therefore, must be a realistic process that is both judicious and creative in what it selects. The fact that something is used in the liturgy does not automatically destroy its previous cultural meaning. On the other hand, the missionary history of the Church is replete with examples of creative liturgical inculturation. Conversion of heart and incompatibility with the faith are reliable but delicate guidelines for inculturation, as that same history will attest.

Historical examples from the past and present are not difficult to find. An interesting part of the initiation rite in some early accounts is the offering of a cup of milk and honey to the newly baptized just before their reception of their first eucharist. Although some have found the origin for this rite in scriptural allusions, Roman pagan culture used this same ritual for newborn infants to ward off sickness and evil spirits and the mystery religions offered a similar drink to their neophytes.[18] One could say that there were some pagan associations with the rite but none which suggested infidelity or incompatibility. In *The Apostolic Tradition*, as Chupungco points out, Hippolytus suggests that the bishop explain the meaning of the rite as the fulfilment of God's promise to the covenant people to lead them into a land of milk and honey. In commenting on the creative inculturation of these early liturgists, Chupungco says:

> They were pastors and catechists who had a keen perception of how their people lived their lives in the cultural milieu of the time. They were profoundly cognizant of their people's ritual needs and aspirations. These were introduced into the liturgy so that the liturgy would not be divorced from the reality of human life. They were great liturgists, because they were pastors.[19]

No better commentary could be offered on the guidelines of the Catechism.

The Catechism does not go into specific questions about or examples of culture and inculturation. This is as it should be. The national catechisms of particular cultural groups, however, should reflect an awareness of how their own cultural situation helps and hinders the living of the gospel and the praise of their saving God. The Catechism rightly points to the Church's vocation both to integrate and to purify the 'authentic riches of culture' (1202) in her mission to the world. Some practical corollaries emerge from such tasks. First, the local Church must ask, from time to time, how its liturgical life is having an impact on its culture. In post-industrial societies, for example, where Sunday is a time for

doing what cannot be done during the week, how do liturgical celebrations help retrieve a sense of the Lord's day and its
redemptive meaning?

Second, does the liturgical life of the local Church prophetically challenge assumed cultural values? Consumerism,
for example, is a cultural trait of many First-World countries.
Yet this cultural disease allows many Christians to ignore the
need of others, since they feel excused by uncontested cultural habits. Worship should be productive of some
countercultural attitudes that challenge such habits.[20] If the
catechisms are to propose the liturgical life and the moral
values in convincing and prophetic ways to Christians of any
age, they must have a keen pastoral sense, as Chupungco
indicated earlier, of their own culture's strength and weaknesses.

Sense of time – the liturgical challenge

One of the most obvious and subtle examples of culture is a
sense of time. Americans, for example, are often characterized by their frenetic sense of time. By comparison,
Mediterranean countries are sometimes judged to have a
fairly relaxed sense of time, at least by Anglo-Saxon standards. From what we are learning about early cultures, there
seems to have always been a compelling need to make certain
times special (e.g., the agricultural feasts of new harvests,
etc.) because they were important to those cultures for religious, sexual or economic reasons.

In the Hebrew and the Christian scriptures, there are also
some indications of a cultural sense of time, but it is challenged and transformed by an acute awareness of time as
God's creation. Time is not cyclical but rather linear, moving
toward the end of creation and time, as we know it. In the
New Testament, the death and resurrection of Christ completely transforms the Christian sense of time. The Christian
community waits in time 'until . . .'. As noted in an earlier
chapter, this 'until' is a practical awareness of being caught in
between the present time and the future reign of God already

coming toward us. Paul's central teaching in this matter, as noted earlier, is that God's future must change the way we live in the present. Our text emphasizes the idea of a 'fixed feast', that is a recurring celebration that 'bears the imprint of the newness of the mystery of Christ' (1164).

When the Catechism, often citing Vatican II, speaks of the liturgical seasons and year, it presumes this sense of time. Otherwise, its claims and demands might seem naïve, if not extravagant: 'In the course of the year ... she unfolds the whole mystery of Christ ... Thus recalling the mysteries of the redemption, she opens up to the faithful the riches of her Lord's powers and merits, so that these are in some way made present in every age' (1163). Throughout this commentary on the Catechism, the paschal mystery of Christ's dying and rising for us has been cited as the sole basis of our worship as a new covenant people. It is not enough that this happened in a saving past time, it must be present to us. This is the uniqueness of the Judaeo-Christian sense of time – a saving past actualized in the present.

This notion of a transformed present is caught in the word 'today', a word that echoes the psalms and prayers of Christ and the early Christian communities, a word that is given new life in the prayers and theology of Leo the Great. 'This "today" of the living God which man is called to enter is "the hour" of Jesus' Passover, which reaches across and underlies all history' (1165). The liturgical result of this theology is, first of all, the celebration of the 'Lord's Day' or Sunday, whose origin is found in the day of Christ's resurrection.[21] Since this day symbolizes the paschal mystery, it must be at the centre of the Christian community's life, 'the pre-eminent day for the liturgical assembly' (1167).

The observant reader will notice that the Catechism has a much larger view of the significance of Sunday than many Catholics. It is not simply a 'day of obligation' or even a day when Mass is celebrated. The Lord's Day is a symbolic time in which the Christian community really enters into the mystery of their salvation in a privileged way. The word of God and the eucharist frame the meaning of their lives in terms of

God's past and present love for them and God's future promise as a focus for their lives. It should be the occasion 'when we ponder, O Christ, the marvels accomplished on this day' (1167, part of the Syriac Office).

Historically Sunday was the original feast. The liturgical year gradually developed with the celebration of the Easter Triduum and eventually other feasts connected with Christ, Mary, the martyrs, and other saints. The development of Holy Week and Lent from the original celebration of Easter is an intriguing and complex history. The limited purpose of the Catechism at this point is to insist on Easter, the 'Feast of feasts', as the heart of the liturgical year because it 'permeates with its powerful energy our old time, until all is subjected to him' (1169). All the other feasts that celebrate the incarnation (such as Christmas and Epiphany) are unified by the paschal mystery (1171). The feasts of the martyrs and the other saints propose examples of how that same mystery has transformed the lives of people like ourselves (1173).

Even when daily eucharist was not always possible, the consecration of time by regular hours of prayer was valued since this practice also celebrated the redeeming death and resurrection of Christ for our sakes. The Catechism emphasizes the link between the baptismal priesthood of all the faithful and praying the 'hours'. As Vatican II had done, it urges those in pastoral ministries to make such prayer accessible to people in parishes (1174–1175). The office of the hours is an integration of several styles of prayer: psalms, hymns, the word of God and responses. The liturgy of the hours complements the eucharist as a communal expression of thanksgiving (1178).[22]

There is always a pastoral purpose that accompanies these celebrations of the paschal mystery in all its aspects. At the same time that we are invited to enter into this mystery, the practical question of our own use of time is challenged by the lives of Christ, Mary and the saints which were also measured by days and years. The Catechism's statement that 'the economy of salvation is at work within the framework of time' (1168) is verified in the feasts celebrated in the eucharist and in the liturgy of the hours. There is the further assurance that the Passover of Jesus and the gift of the Holy Spirit has ushered in the initial experience of the reign of God in our time (1168). In other words, the liturgy is the best teacher of God's sense of time, that is, the reasons why we are given time and the courage to live as pilgrims in that time.

Once again, the Catechism has presented the classical Christian meaning of time: with Christ's death we need no longer be slaves to time but are empowered to shape that time to the work of Christ and to look forward to a 'time that is not a time'. In each historical epoch, however, Christians have had to confront and challenge their cultural sense of time in order to live out this belief. Even neighbouring cultures do not share exactly the same sense of time. There-fore, in 'translating' the message of the Catechism on liturgical time into the cultural situation of a country, some questions should be asked.

First, how sharp a distinction is there between the 'public' and 'private' sense of time in this culture? 'Public' time refers to the time expended in our social and work lives, time that is no longer our own but controlled by other people or imper-sonal factors. The time it takes to commute to work might serve as one example. It is not uncommon for people to spend two to four hours (or longer) in getting to and from work. Commuters are at the mercy of outside forces such as traffic delays, weather, mechanical failures, and even occa-sional violence. The sense of time one has in commuting is not the same as 'private' time. Private times are buffer zones in which we attempt to have some momentary relief from the public demands made on our time by work, school, social obligations, and so on. We speak of 'quality' time with our families and friends because it is often denied us by other competing 'times' in our lives.[23]

Liturgy requires a balance between these two senses of time. Public time has become a negative term and experience for many contemporary people. But, as we noted in an earlier chapter, 'liturgy in the world' attempts to restore a Christian sense of purpose to time spent in all the forums of human life and activity. Public time in the best sense of the term is the liturgy for the sake of the world and its salvation. Private time, on the other hand, does not mean privatized time, that is, a selfish hoarding of time for our own pursuits. The cultural temptation after a busy week may be to withhold time from others. Liturgy invites us to expend time not only on praise of God but on care of others. Liturgy may well encourage a countercultural sense of time.

Second, does the culture encourage a manipulation of time and expectations that distort a Christian sense of time? The liturgical year, as we have seen, encourages a realistic sense of time because it helps to clarify the purpose and goals of time from God's viewpoint. Christ's incarnation redefined time by the way in which he spent his life in the service of others and laid down his life for the sake of others. A closer examination of the cultural sense of time in some First-World countries might reveal a very different sense of time.

One example is the manipulation, that is, the distortion, of time in the audiovisual world. Television regularly presents story lines that must fit into the artificial constraints of commercial breaks throughout a 30- or 60-minute pro-gramme. As one critic notes, 'As a result, situations that in real life develop naturally over varying periods receive a standard, short, artificial treatment in television. Television regularizes our experience, encouraging us to think of the serious and the trivial as equally important in terms of time, if not in the mind's eye.'[24] Younger generations who are accus-tomed to allocating large segments of the week to television viewing have formed their cultural sense of time, in part, by such manipulation. When these people step into a Sunday liturgy or hear an explanation of liturgical time, they cannot be expected to put aside temporarily such cultural formation. Those who teach and celebrate the liturgy can begin to address the problem by recognizing it as such. Liturgical time does have something to say to these young people but it must begin with the sense of time they already have.

Unreal sociocultural expectations also contribute to the sense of time. In upwardly mobile cultures, for example, parents often have unrealistic expectations of their children. In some segments of society, these expectations are projected on children even in pre-school years when they are placed in 'prep' kindergartens that guarantee more easy entry into the 'right' primary school, leading to the 'right' secondary school, and so on. As a result, their parents' expectations may distort the young person's sense of time by unreasonable or even unhealthy pressures to succeed. Liturgical time is on a collision course with such notions of time because even the most laudable ambitions and goals are being measured by different standards.

Where art and worship meet

As mentioned above, we will treat the Catechism's discussion of liturgical music (1156–1158), images (1159–1162), and architecture (1179–1186) together since they are important cultural expressions transformed by a religious purpose. Although the term 'sacred art' is a broader term than that of 'liturgical art', the Catechism's section on the former (2500–2503) may serve as an insightful preface to the latter. Within the context of a theology of creation, truth, goodness, and beauty are discussed as revelatory of God the Creator (2500). Art gives 'form to the truth of reality in a language accessible to sight or hearing' (2501). The form of sacred art should reflect its goal: praising the transcendent mystery of God made visible in Christ (2502).

Music seems to have been a heritage of the Christian community from the very beginning (see Eph 5:19), though not all of it may have been used liturgically. Gregorian chant, the medieval organum Masses and the polyphonic Masses of the fifteenth and sixteenth centuries were composed for liturgical use and constitute some of the high points in the history of Western music. In the past, the Church has been an important patron of the arts, but more especially of liturgical art in all its forms.

On the other hand, because of its complexity much of this music had to be sung by highly capable musicians, thus preventing the community's rightful participation in the liturgy. The Catechism, therefore, offers three criteria for liturgical music: 'beauty expressive of prayer, the unanimous participation of the assembly at the designated moments, and the solemn character of the celebration' (1157). Such music will be further enhanced to the degree that it reflects 'the *cultural richness* of the People of God who celebrate' (1158, emphasis in the text). (One might argue, for example, about the liturgical appropriateness of the musical settings of the Mass by Haydn and Mozart, but they are exceptional witnesses to the cultural heritage of Catholics in the Austro-Hungarian empire.) Finally, the texts of such music should usually derive from the scriptures and liturgical sources.

Sacred images also seem to have a long history in the Church. In fact, the Church has had to defend the use of images (the Catechism has two citations (1160–1161) from the Council of Nicaea II in defence of such images). The incarnation of Jesus Christ brought about a 'new "economy" of images' (1159) since God has been made visible in his Son. Over the centuries for largely illiterate populations such images were an important teacher of the gospels. Sacred images should complement and enrich the liturgy 'so that the mystery celebrated is imprinted in the heart's memory and is then expressed in the new life of the faithful' (1162).

The early Christian communities assembled for worship either in open places or in house churches, that is, homes used regularly for such purposes. Therefore, it is not surprising that the Catechism begins its brief discussion of liturgical architecture by reminding us that it is the gathered community that is a 'spiritual house' (1179). Church buildings 'make visible the Church living in this place' (1180). As with the other sacred arts, liturgical architecture has a long history, beginning with the Roman basilicas and continuing into the twentieth century with the contemporary chapel of Ronchamp by Le Corbusier (built in 1955).

The Catechism contents itself with citing Vatican II's direction that the church should be in good taste and fit for prayer and liturgy (1181). (These initial conciliar directions have since been given more precision in several important directives on church architecture.[25]) This is followed by a concise explanation of the significance of the tabernacle, the liturgical oils, the presider's chair, the lectern, baptistery, and the penance and reconciliation room (1182–1185) and the general requirement that the church be a space that encourages prayer that prolongs and helps internalize the eucharistic celebrations.

Finally, the Catechism gives another important characteristic of a church that is too often forgotten: it is a symbol of the kingdom of God (1186). To enter a church is to cross a threshold 'which symbolizes passing from the world wounded by sin to the world of the new Life to which all men are called'. The church, then, reminds us of our ultimate destination and that, since God has called all people to salvation, the church is 'the house of *all* God's children, open and welcoming' (1186, emphasis in text). This last remark sums up a history of the church as sanctuary for the outcast and the pursued even to our own days.

Concluding remarks

The Catechism offers the universal Church a fairly rich theology in liturgy in a highly compact form. One might say that for each line of the printed text there are volumes of theological research and reflection as a subtext. We have tried to supply some of the theological context for the discussion on the liturgy in the Catechism. Toward the end of the Catechism one final precis of this theology is offered:

> In the sacramental liturgy of the Church, the mission of Christ and of the Holy Spirit proclaims, makes present and communicates the mystery of salvation which is continued in the heart that prays ... Prayer internalizes and assimilates the liturgy during and after its celebration. Even when lived out 'in secret', prayer is always *prayer of the Church*; it is a communion with the Holy Trinity. (2655, emphasis in text)

This highly condensed paragraph represents not only a theological summary but also a challenge to the pastoral ministries of each local Church.

At the very beginning of the Catechism, each local Church was reminded of the 'indispensable adaptations' that are required 'by the differences of culture, age, spiritual maturity, and social and ecclesial condition among all those to whom it is addressed' (24). With this admonition in mind, let me offer three suggestions. First, the Catechism speaks of what God is already doing in our midst. Therefore, the religious experience of the local Church and its individual members should be valued, evoked and addressed when speaking of the reasons for and the manner of their worship. Second, each local Church has a cultural wealth that can contextualize the teaching of the Catechism and make relevant what otherwise might seem theoretical. The Catechism reminds us of the importance of communications in cultural formation (2493) and the same might be said of liturgical formation.[26]

Finally, Aylward Shorter has provided a challenge to all who teach the faith: 'Inculturation is not merely a dialogue between Gospel and culture, it is the Gospel bringing into existence a new cultural creation.'[27] As we approach the second millennium, who would question the urgent need that this gospel task be carried on with new conviction and hope?

Notes

1 Bishops' Committee on the Liturgy, *Music in Catholic Worship* (Washington, DC; United States Catholic Conference, 1972), p. 1.

2 R. May, *Love and Will* (New York: W. W. Norton, 1969), p. 234: author's emphasis.

3 Augustine, *On Baptism, Against the Donatists:* translation in *Nicene and Post-Nicene Fathers of the Christian Church,* vol. IV, ed. P. Schaff (Grand Rapids, MI: W. B. Eerdmans, 1979), pp. 466–7.

4 P. Brown, *The Cult of the Saints* (Chicago: University of Chicago, 1981), pp. 55–6.

5 K. Rahner, 'On the theology of worship' in *Theological Investigations,* vol. XIX (New York: Crossroad/London: Darton, Longman and Todd, 1983), pp. 141–9.

6 Ibid., p. 147.

7 Francis of Assisi, 'Canticle of Brother Sun' in *Francis and Clare: The Complete Works,* ed. R. Armstrong and I. Brady (New York: Paulist Press, 1982), p. 38.

8 C. Geertz, *The Interpretation of Cultures* (New York: Basic Books, 1973), p. 89, emphasis added.

9 Ibid., p. 12.

10 Ibid., p. 90.

11 Vatican II, Pastoral Constitution on the Church in the Modern World, *Gaudium et spes* 53. For a thorough discussion see A. Shorter, *Toward a Theology of Inculturation* (London: Geoffrey Chapman/Maryknoll, NY: Orbis Books, 1988).

12 This is exemplified in two very different responses of the Church to the cultural challenge of a particular situation. In the case of the evangelization of the Slavic peoples by Sts Cyril and Methodius in the ninth century, Pope John VII eventually allowed the liturgy to be translated into the vernacular. In the case of the so-called 'Chinese rites' controversy, Rome eventually decided against the Jesuits' appeal for incorporating some aspects of Chinese reverence for ancestors and other cultural elements into the liturgy. This ruling was finally changed by Pius XII. For a history of this latter debate, see G. Minamiki, *The Chinese Rites Controversy from Its Beginning to Modern Times* (Chicago: Loyola University, 1985).

13 Vatican II, *Ad Gentes* (Decree on the Church's Missionary Activity) 22.

14 John Paul II, 'One Church, many cultures' in *The Church and Culture Since Vatican II,* ed. J. Gremillion (Notre Dame, IN: University of Notre Dame, 1985), p. 215. The same collection has five other addresses of the Pope on the question of culture and faith: pp. 162–222.

15 A. Chupungco, *Liturgies of the Future* (New York: Paulist Press, 1989), p. 29.

16 For the differences between adaptation, acculturation, and inculturation and other such terms, see A. Chupungco, *Liturgical Inculturation* (New York: Pueblo, 1992), pp. 13–27.

17 See A. Chupungco, *Beyond Inculturation* (Washington, DC: Pastoral Press, 1994).

18 Ibid., pp. 11–12.

19 Ibid., p. 12.

20 I have discussed this at length in *The American Emmaus: Faith and Sacrament in the American Culture* (New York: Crossroad, 1995).

21 The Catechism, citing the Byzantine liturgy, notes that 'The day of Christ's Resurrection is both the first day of the week, the memorial of

the first day of creation, and the "eighth day", on which Christ after his "rest" on the great sabbath inaugurates the "day the Lord has made", the "day that knows no evening" ' (1166).

22 See R. Taft, *The Liturgy of the Hours in East and West* (Collegeville, MN: Liturgical Press, 1986), pp. 331–65.

23 See J. Rifkin, *Time Wars: The Primary Conflict in Human History* (New York: H. Holt, 1986).

24 R. M. Mereleman, *Making Something of Ourselves* (Berkeley: University of California, 1984), p. 92. His whole chapter on 'Television: structure vs. culture', pp. 70–115, bears reading.

25 One example for the Church in the United States is authored by The Bishops' Committee on the Liturgy: *Environment and Art in Catholic Worship* (Washington, DC: National Catholic Conference of Bishops, 1978).

26 For an approach that might be adapted to this cultural formation, see G. Ostdiek, *Catechesis for Liturgy* (Washington, DC: Pastoral Press, 1986).

27 Shorter, *Toward a Theology of Inculturation*, p. 263.